A Brief Survey of
AUSTRIAN HISTORY

A Brief Survey of
AUSTRIAN HISTORY

By Richard Rickett

GEORG PRACHNER VERLAG
IN WIEN

Illustration on the jacket:
Prince Eugene of Savoy, Prince Karl Franz of Lorraine and Duke Karl V. of Lorraine after
the victory over the Turks at Mount Harsany 1687, Lithograph by Franz Gerasch after a
painting by Wilhelm Camphausen, in the possession of the Austrian National Library

Seventh edition 1983

ISBN 3-85367-001-6
© Copyright 1966
By Georg Prachner Verlag in Vienna
Cover design by Herbert Schiefer
maps by Willi Bahner
Printed by Salzer - Ueberreuter in Vienna
Printed in Austria
All illustrations with kind permission
of the Austrian National Library

CONTENTS

FOREWORD

Obviously, for a foreigner to agree to write the history of a country he hopes to go on being allowed to live in is asking for trouble. My only excuse is the thousands of English-speaking tourists who year after year patiently absorb information and statistics from expert and highly-qualified guides, yet have only the haziest idea (though they dare not admit as much in front of the others) of who all the illustrious personages referred to actually were. It is to English-speaking visitors who want to get the most out of all they see and are shown during their stay in Austria that this book is conscientiously and in all humility dedicated.

R. R.

CHAPTER ONE

Celts, Romans and Babenbergs

750–400 B. C.	The "Hallstatt" Civilisation (early Iron Age).
279 B.C.	Celtic invasion.
150 B.C.	The Celts establish the Kingdom of Noricum with its centre in present-day Carinthia.
101 B.C.	The invading Cimbri and Teutoni routed by the Roman general Caius Marius.
15 B.C.	Establishment of the Roman Province of Rhaetia, including North Tyrol and Vorarlberg.
10 A.D.	Under the Roman Emperor Augustus the Romans take over Noricum and establish the Province of Pannonia.
25 A.D.	Under the Roman Emperor Tiberius a Roman frontier (the "Limes") is consolidated along the Danube from Castra Boiorum (Passau) to Carnuntum.
100 A.D.	Establishment of the Roman camp of Vindobona.
180 A.D.	Death of the Roman Emperor Marcus Aurelius at Vindobona.
304 A.D.	*Christianity reaches the Danube and in 313 is declared by the Roman Emperor Constantine to be the State Religion.*
375 A.D.	Start of the great Migrations. Carnuntum obliterated.
434–53	The Huns under Attila overrun Pannonia but withdraw on his death.
488	Completion of Roman withdrawal from the entire Danube area. Infiltration of Slavs and Avars from the East.
700	*St. Rupert founds the Benedictine Abbey of St. Peter on the ruins of Juvavum (Salzburg).*
ca. 740	*St. Rupert's Church in Vienna.*
791–99	Charlemagne wipes out the Avars and forms the "Ostmark", Vienna becoming a border fortress.
800	Charlemagne crowned in Rome as "Roman Emperor of the West".
881	Battle between the Franks and the Magyars at "Wenia" (first mention of the original version of "Wien").
907	Battle of Pressburg (Bratislava) leads to the disintegration of Charlemagne's "Ostmark".

955	The Magyars defeated by Otto the Great at the Battle of Lechfeld. Reconstitution of the "Ostmark".
962	Otto is crowned by the Pope in Rome, the first Holy Roman Emperor.
976	The Babenbergs acquire "Austria".
996	First appeerence of the word "Ostarrichi" in a document drawn up by the Emperor Otto III.
1070–1180	Building of Hohensalzburg Fortress in Salzburg.
1095–1136	Babenberg ruler Leopold III "the Holy" establishes his residence on what is now the Leopoldsberg.
ca. 1137	Vienna a fortified city. *Reconstruction of St. Peter's at Salzburg and (thirty yaers later) of the Cathedral. Building of Gurk Cathedral and Millstatt Monastery in Carinthia, and of Seckau Monastery in Styria.*
1147	*Work begun on the Romanesque Church of St. Stephen of Vienna.*
1156	Under Babenberg ruler Heinrich II "Jasomirgott" Austria is elevated by the Emperor Friedrich Barbarossa to the status of a hereditary Duchy.
1191	Babenberg ruler Leopold V participates in the Third Crusade. King Richard I of England imprisoned at Dürnstein on the Danube.
1225	Dominicans and Franciscans settle in Vienna.
1246	Death of the last Babenberg Friedrich II "the Quarrelsome" at the Battle of the Leitha against the Magyars.
1246–73	The "Terrible Interregnum": anarchy and confusion.
1251	Vienna is seized by King Ottocar Premysl of Bohemia.
1259	*Work on the Romanesque west front of St. Stephen's Church in Vienna.*
1273	Count Rudolf of Habsburg is crowned "German King" at Aachen.
1276	Ottocar Premysl forced by Rudolf to withdraw from Vienna.
1278	Rudolf finally defeats Ottocar at the Battle of the Marchfeld, in which Ottocar is killed. Beginning of 640 years of Habsburg rule in Austria.
1282	Rudolf and Albrecht Habsburg are awarded the Duchy of Austria (Upper and Lower Austria), Styria, Carinthia and Carniola, and reallocate them in the following year.

Tracing the dawn of history in the area now occupied by the Republic of Austria is a process of groping about in the mists of antiquity, which every now and again lift for a moment or two to disclose glimpses of the Stone and Bronze Ages, as evidenced by excavations along the Danube and in Carinthia, and by the discovery of urn-fields in Tyrol and Styria.

In the beginning was salt. The earliest Austrian civilisation which can be reconstructed in considerable detail is the so-called "Hallstatt" civilisation, as revealed by the burial-grounds near Hallstatt in Upper Austria dating from the early Iron Age. The prosperity of Hallstatt was based on salt, which was also mined at Dürrnberg near Hallein in the Province of Salzburg, Salzburg itself being the trading centre of a whole area, later known as the "Salzkammergut", reserved for the mining and exploitation of salt.

During the Celtic incursions that culminated in about 279 B.C. the salt-mines are known to have been efficiently operated by the invaders, who gradually extended their hold on the area until by 150 B.C. they had established a Kingdom of Noricum comprising roughly present-day Upper Austria south of the Danube, Salzburg, West Styria and Carinthia, the Romans having been forced to withdraw southwards. But the Romans were well aware of the commercial importance of this area, and first by peaceful penetration and later by force gradually ousted the Celts. Prospectors and Consuls from Rome secured a goodly share of the iron, salt and wine trades, the two main traffic arteries being the east-west Danube and the north-south "Amber Road" from Jutland to Rome via the Semmering Pass, along which whale-tusks and amber (picturesquely described as "the tears of the sea") from the north were traded against bronze swords and oil-pitchers, for instance, from the south.

Little by little the Romans re-asserted themselves and in 102 and 101 B.C. the military genius of the great Roman commander Caius Marius annihilated first the Teutoni and then the Cimbri. Delivered from the threat of barbarian incursions from the north the area was thoroughly colonised, the twin hallmarks of Roman civilisation being Roman baths and Roman roads. Under the Emperor Augustus the Province of Rhaetia, including what is now North Tyrol and Vorarlberg, was established after prolonged and stubborn resistance, and shortly afterwards Noricum was incorporated into the Roman Empire. The Romans further consolidated their authority along the Danube by establishing the Province of Pannonia, which stretched from the eastern frontier of Noricum to roughly the site of present-day Budapest; and under the next Emperor Tiberius work was started in 25. A.D. on strengthening Augustus' "Limes", the Danube frontier, against the Barbarian hordes to the north.

As for the Danube, the Greeks, although uncertain as to its origin, had been familiar with its estuary. To its lower reaches, made familiar by the Argonauts, they gave the name of Ister, first referred to by Herodotus in 450 B.C. In the first century B.C. there were Macedonian settlements along the south bank, but the Celtic incursions deprived the Danube of the benefits of Graeco-Roman civilisation for many hundreds of years. Eventually however the Romans, as we have seen, fought their way back to the Danube lands, subjugating the Germanic inhabitants and setting up powerful military bases. They also discovered the source of the Danube, the upper reaches of which they called "Danubius". In time they thrust downstream, first to Ulm and later to Regensburg, Passau and Carnuntum. They divided the entire Danube valley into three military areas, each equipped with a river flotilla of its own. The two most important military bases were Passau (Castra Boiorum) and Vienna (Vindobona). Watch-towers were erected within sight of each other all along the river, and river

craft were constantly on patrol. Whereas Julius Caesar had
made the Rhine his frontier, Augustus ordered a fortified
"Limes" for the protection of the vital Danube waterway.
The river's upper reaches were protected by a fortified
military road from Lake Constance to the "Limes". From
Ulm right down to the Black Sea there was a regular service
of river vessels linking the towns with the Roman frontier fortifications. All questions of trade and navigation
were subordinated to strategic and military considerations.
What with the transport of legions and of supplies for
the military bases and observations posts on the right
bank, not to mention the shipments of corn from the
Danube Provinces and Colonies for storage in the great
granaries, the Danube became an indispensable line of
communication. But towards the end of the 4th century
the Romans lost one position after another, and apart from
its brief occupation by the Huns from 430—454 the Danube
became part of the Germanic territories. It was not until
the early part of the 9th century that it regained some importance as a navigable waterway. Later, the Crusades
brought a further increase in its traffic, but from the 13th
century the importance of the Danube gradually declined
and the capture of Constantinople by the Turks brought
traffic between the upper and lower reaches to a complete
standstill.

The history of the various nations along the river's
course has left its traces. It was along the Danube that
Charlemagne created his "Eastern March", the kernel
which eventually swelled into the vast Austro-Hungarian
Monarchy. The "beautiful blue Danube" has witnessed
many fateful chapters in Europe's history; and the famous
Nibelung saga tells how in the fabulous days of yore Kriem-
hild and her retinue passed down the Danube to the land
of Etzel (Attila), King of the Huns, the "Scourge of God",
and perished there. Centuries later the great Prince Eugene
of Savoy left his mark on the river's history by ordering

the building of a bridge near Belgrade and by finally averting the Turkish menace.

But to return to the Romans. The chief town (municipium) at the eastern end of the "Limes" was Carnuntum, some ruins of which can still be seen near the town of Hainburg on the road from Vienna to Bratislava. It seems to have been a predominantly civilian community, with luxurious baths and two amphitheatres, one seating about 13,000, though there was also a military camp set up by Tiberius in 25 A.D. as a base for forays across the Danube (which in point of fact were seldom if ever ventured). Carnuntum was also the residence of the Roman Governor of Pannonia. Among the military defences of the "Limes" was the strongly fortified "municipium" of Vindobona on a broad plateau at the top of a slope running down to the Danube in the oldest part of what is now the Inner City, not far from the church of Maria am Gestade. The course of one of its moats on the southern side was identical with that of the present Graben, and the military area also included what is now Am Hof and the Hoher Markt, its eastern boundary being the Rotenturmstrasse. Vindobona was intended as a military stronghold at one of the weakest points of the "Limes", and one of the crack legions was permanently stationed there. It was at Vindobona too that the great Roman Emperor and Stoic philosopher Marcus Aurelius died after unflinchingly enduring eight winter campaigns on the frozen banks of the Danube against the Marcommani, who together with their allies the Quadi were threatening to overrun the frontier from Bohemia. The fact that Vindobona was also the chief base of the Roman Danube flotillas requires a word or two of explanation.

The ships lay at anchor in what is now the Danube Canal, but in former times the "Canal" was only one of the numerous arms into which the Danube split up just north of Vienna, so that to the east of the Inner City (Vindobona) there was an area of low-lying isolated meadows amid arms

14

of the river. Eventually the largest of these meadows were linked by bridges, and the area between the main stream and the widest of the arms (now the Canal) was built upon. It was not until the Danube Regulation Scheme of 1868—1875 that the various arms were diverted into the present broad main stream to the north and east of the city, and the marshy ground was drained. So the answer to the question so frequently asked: "Why isn't Vienna right on the Danube like Budapest?" is that in former times the Danube at Vienna was not the single broad stream that it is at Budapest, and that Vienna did in fact grow up along its largest arm.

Christianity was declared the official religion of Rome in 313, having reached the Danube about ten years earlier. The principal dioceses in what is now Austria were at Aguntum in East Tyrol, Teurnia in northern Carinthia, and Virunum near Klagenfurt. One of the most assiduous propagators of the new religion was St. Severin, after whom the Viennese suburb of Sievering is said to be named. By about 375 the Danube area, from time immemorial the crossroads of Europe, was inevitably overrun during the Great Migrations by milling hordes of Vandals, Goths, Huns, Teutons, Slavs and Franks, all on the move. Carnuntum was engulfed in the flood and never rose again, but Vindobona, which in 453 appears in a document as "Vindominia", served as a welcome sanctuary to all of Celtic-Roman descent.

From about 400 onwards the Romans gradually withdrew from the Danube area as a result of incessant pressure from the barbarians to the north, the evacuation being completed by 488, twelve years after the end of the Western Roman Empire. The vacuum was immediately filled by the Huns, who poured into Pannonia from the east but later withdrew on the death of their King Attila, the "Scourge of God". In their wake came confused masses of Slavs, Avars

15

and Magyars from the East, Teutons from the North and Bajuvars from the West, all hoping for a share of the Roman heritage. Yet it was during this time of turmoil and confusion that two of Austria's earliest Christian monuments were founded, St. Rupert's Benedictine Abbey of St. Peter in Salzburg and St. Rupert's Church in Vienna (about 740).

Very gradually Christianity and the South German Bajuvarians, after asserting themselves in the west, pushed eastwards down the Danube until there finally emerged the Empire of the Franks under its redoubtable leader Charlemagne, who succeeded in uniting Germanic and Christian interests and influences. After incorporating Carinthia in 788 Charlemagne concentrated all his forces against the Avars, whom he virtually wiped out. As an eastern bulwark he set up the "Ostmark", bounded by the rivers Enns, Raab and Drau; and Vienna became a Carolingian-Frankish border fortress. Charlemagne's "Ostmark" lasted until about 880, when following a battle between the Franks and the Magyars at "Wenia" (Vindobona) the western forces were defeated at the Battle of Pressburg (now Bratislava) in 907 and the "Ostmark" collapsed — for the time being. Revenge came in 955, when Otto the Great routed the Magyars at the Battle of Lechfeld and reconstituted the "Ostmark" as a bulwark against them. Seven years later, in 962, Otto was crowned by the Pope in Rome, and the Holy Roman Empire made its appearance on the pages of history and remained there for the next eight hundred and forty-four years.

It has been observed, somewhat spitefully, that the Holy Roman Empire was neither holy nor Roman nor an Empire, but seeing that it had an Emperor for nearly 850 years, and that the Emperor was originally crowned by the Pope in Rome, the title can hardly be described as fanciful. Although Otto was the first Holy Roman Emperor as such, the Empire really dated from Charlemagne's coronation in Rome on Christmas Day 800 as Roman Emperor of the West, a title that had been extinct since the days of Odoacer more than 300 years earlier. It was a splendid gesture by the Pope, an attempt to obliterate memories of the Dark Ages, to distract people's minds from the hardships and uncertainties of the times by a manifestation that the great days of Augustus and Marcus Aurelius had returned. It was a blend of temporal and spiritual power, an aspiration to unite the sanctity of the Pope with the organising power of Rome, to combine feudalism with justice. As such it was based on sentiment, but on assuming the crown Otto did in fact wield a power that was derived partly from the Pope and partly from the military resources of the domains that owed allegiance to him. The fact that such a vast, loosely-knit organisation survived as long as it did shows that the Holy Roman Empire was more than just a pathetic attempt to put the clock back. And one of its greatest assets was its continuity: after 1440 the crown of the Holy Roman Empire was invariably worn by a Habsburg, apart from a very brief period at the beginning of Maria Theresia's reign; not by any right, privilege or monopoly, but by election. Up till 1806 the title Emperor is to be taken as meaning the Holy Roman Emperor, simultaneously Archduke of Austria and later King of Bohemia and Hungary. It was not until the Emperor Franz renounced the crown of the Holy Roman Empire in 1806, thereby bringing the institution to an end, that he created for himself the title of Emperor of Austria.

The year 976 is an important milestone in Austrian history: the Holy Roman Emperor Otto II presented Margrave Leopold of Babenberg with the south-eastern territories as a reward for his help in crushing a Bavarian revolt. The Babenberg dynasty ruled Austria for the next 270 years, until 1246. Starting from the Wachau district of the Danube the Babenbergs gradually moved their capital eastwards from the Pöchlarn area to Melk, where the second Babenberg Heinrich I (994—1018) founded a monastery, and then to Tulln and Klosterneuburg. Legend has it that Leopold III "the Holy" (1095—1136, perhaps the outstanding member of this outstanding dynasty), built himself a castle on what is now the Leopoldsberg. Finally, it was left to Heinrich II (1141—1177), nicknamed ,,Jasomirgott" because of his fondness for this particular oath, ("So help me God": there is a street named after him leading off the Stephansplatz in Vienna) to establish his capital in Vienna at what is now "Am Hof". It was during his rule, in 1156 to be exact, that "Austria" was given the special status of a hereditary Duchy within the Holy Roman Empire by the Emperor Friedrich Barbarossa, in return for renouncing claims to Bavaria.

The era of the Babenbergs was a time of great prosperity. They seem to have been wise and far-seeing rulers who exploited the natural resources of their domains, particularly gold, silver and salt, and at the same time paid due attention to spiritual matters. Among the great monasteries that were founded in those days are Melk (1000), Göttweig (1074), Klosterneuburg (1114), Heiligenkreuz (1135), Admont in Styria (1074), and Millstatt in Carinthia (1070). They also established a chain of redoubtable castles and defensive fortifications against inroads from the east and north. By 1137 Vienna itself was a fortified city, and 10 years later work was started on a Romanesque Basilica dedicated to St. Stephen just outside the south-eastern corner of the old Roman Vindobona. As the Basilica took shape, a new quarter, mainly commercial, sprang up, peopled by merchants anxious to take advantage of the Babenberg "boom". They were well aware that the prosperity of the Babenberg domains was based on firm rule and (not for the last time in Austria's history) astute dynastic marriages, so that the Babenbergs may justly claim to

18

have shaped what was eventually to emerge as "Austria". It was also during their rule, in 996, that the word "Ostar-richi" appeared for the first time in a document drawn up by the Holy Roman Emperor.

But the sky was not entirely cloudless. Throughout the 270 years of its tenure the Babenberg dynasty was constantly beset by three preoccupations: the chronic quarrels be-tween the Pope and the Holy Roman Emperor, the menace of the Bohemians and Magyars, and the Crusades. Which brings us to the romantic story of Leopold V "the Vir-tuous" (1177—1194) and King Richard I of England, the only excuse for re-telling such a well-known tale being its association with the Austrian scene.

In 1190, during the Third Crusade, King Richard I of England was deemed by Duke Leopold to have insulted the red-white-red Austrian flag by hauling it down from the ramparts of the captured city of Acre. Attempting to make his way back to England in disguise Richard was recog-nised at Erdberg near Vienna and (so the story goes) imprisoned in Dürnstein castle on the Danube; until one day the troubadour Blondel, whose songs had hitherto elicited no response whatever from castle after castle along the Rhine and Danube, eventually heard his song being taken up and completed from a Dürnstein dungeon. Having found his lord and master Blondel lost no time in procuring his release. It is not known whether Leopold considered the substantial ransom he was paid made up for being excommunicated, which was what happened when the Pope heard about the affair. Probably not.

And so to the last of the Babenbergs, Friedrich II "the Quarrelsome", who after delivering Central Europe from the menace of a vast Mongolian invasion despite being heavily outnumbered, finally indulged in one quarrel too many and was killed in 1246 at a relatively early age on the battlefield of the Leitha, fighting the Magyars. There followed a terrible time of anarchy and upheavals, the so-called "Interregnum" when there was no Emperor and the Duchy's neighbours where poised to pounce on the leaderless domains. The Babenbergs had been good rulers and had steered the Duchy to a high standard of stability and prospertity. From the turmoil of peoples and rulers jostling each other for a share in the spoils of the Babenberg heritage there eventually emerged the redoubtable figure of King Ottocar Premysl of Bohemia, who entered Vienna in 1251 and soon laid hands on Carinthia and Carniola as well. This aroused the anxiety of the Pope as well as of the Emperor, and eventually brought Ottocar into inevitable conflict with a certain Rudolf of Habsburg, who was elected "German King" in 1273, and charged with restoring law and order in the south-east. Gathering forces as he moved eastwards Rudolf entered the Duchy in 1276, and as most of the local leaders flocked to his standard with enthusiasm King Ottocar, encamped on the Marchfeld plain to the east of Vienna, soon found himself (for once) on the defensive. Outmanoeuvred by what in modern military parlance would be called a "pincers movement" between Rudolf and his Hungarian allies to the east Ottocar was forced to withdraw to his Bohemian domains and renounce all his conquests. But not for long: two years later he made a determined bid to restore his fortunes and at the battle of Marchfeld, one of the decisive battles in European history, was utterly defeated by Rudolf and killed on the field of action.

This year 1278 is a turning-point in Austrian history. Rudolf was now undisputed master of the south-east, and at the Diet of Augsburg was awarded what is now Lower and part of Upper Austria, plus the Duchies of Styria and Carniola, for so faithfully discharging the mission he had been entrusted with a few years before. In 1283 Rudolf divided up these territories among the family, his son Albrecht being given Austria and Styria, and Carinthia and Carniola being allotted to Count Meinhard II of Tyrol.

So began the long dominion of the House of Habsburg in Austria, the "Casa d'Austria" that ruled until 1918. The following chapters will show how the dynasty steadily augmented its domains until by the time of the great Charles V (1519—1556) it could boast of ruling an Empire "on which the sun never set", united solely by allegiance to the dynasty. The Habsburg title was: King of Bohemia and Hungary, Archduke of Austria, Duke of Styria, Count of Tyrol, and Lord of Trieste; all this quite apart from the vast dominions of the Spanish branch in the New World as well as in the Old. From now until the disintegration in 1918 the history of Austria is the history of the House of Habsburg, and Rudolf's victory on the Marchfeld in 1278 set the course of European history for the next six hundred and forty years.

CHAPTER TWO

The Early Habsburgs

Austria

1335 Albrecht II acquires Carinthia and Carniola.

1363 Habsburgs acquire first property in Vorarlberg. Margareta Maultasch makes over Tyrol to Rudolf IV.
1365 *Foundation of Vienna University.*

1374 Habsburgs acquire Istria and Friuli (parts).
1375 Counts of Bregenz cede the Bregenzerwald and Feldkirch to the House of Habsburg.
1382 Habsburgs acquire Trieste and more of Vorarlberg.
1394–96 Habsburg feuds and temporary partition of domains.
1433 *Completion of south tower of St. Stephen's Cathedral, Vienna.*
1440–93 Friedrich III, first Habsburg to be crowned Holy Roman Emperor at Rome (in 1452).
1474 With acquisition of Bregenz Habsburgs acquire the whole of Vorarlberg.
1477 Habsburgs acquire Netherlands and Franche-Comté of Burgundy by marriage.

Elsewhere
1328–1400 *Geoffrey Chaucer.*

1348 *Foundation of first German-speaking University at Prague.*

1369–1415 John Huss in Bohemia.

1421 Venice at the height of her power.
1429 Joan of Arc.
1434 Ascendancy of the Medici at Florence until 1527.
1453 The Turks capture Constantinople.

Austria	Elsewhere
1485 Matthias Corvinus, King of Hungary, occupies Vienna until his death in 1490. The Emperor Friedrich III makes his capital at Wiener Neustadt.	1485 End of the Wars of the Roses in England in favour of the Tudors.
	1489 The Queen of Cyprus cedes the island to Venice.
1490 *Michael Pacher's altar at St. Wolfgang, Upper Austria.*	
	1492 Christopher Columbus reaches the New World.
1493–1519 Maximilian I makes his residence at Innsbruck.	
1496 Marriage of Maximilian's son to daughter of Spanish rulers Ferdinand and Isabella.	
1498 *Foundation of the Vienna Hofkapelle.*	1498 Voyages of Vasco da Gama.
1499 Switzerland wrests independence from the Habsburgs.	
1500 *Completion of the "Goldenes Dachl" in Innsbruck.*	
1515 Double marriage of Maximilian's grand children to heirs to Bohemian and Hungarian thrones. "De jure" acquisition in 1526.	
	1519–56 Charles V.
	1520–66 Suleiman the Magnificent expands Ottoman Empire
1521–64 Ferdinand I, the first Habsburg to reside in the Hofburg.	1521 Diet of Worms: Martin Luther excommunicated.
1521 The House of Habsburg separates into two lines, an Austrian and a Spanish.	
1529 First Turkish siege of Vienna.	
	1532 Pizarro's conquest of Peru.
1541 *Death of Paracelsus in Salzburg.*	1541 The Turks capture Budapest.
	1545–63 Council of Trent.
	1546 *Death of Martin Luther.*
	1564 *Death of Michelangelo and birth of Shakespeare.*

Austria	Elsewhere
	1558–1603 The Elizabethan period in England. Voyages of Drake, Raleigh, Frobisher etc.
1570–1640 The Counter Reformation.	1570 The Turks capture Cyprus from Venice.
	1571 Don John of Austria annihilates the Turkish fleet at Lepanto.
1578 *Completion of North Tower of St. Stephen's Cathedral.*	
1580 *Lipizza stud started (Spanish Riding-School).*	
1585 *Foundation of Graz University.*	
1587–1628 *Reconstruction of Salzburg by Archbishops Wolf Dietrich, Marcus Sitticus and Paris Lodron.*	1587 Execution of Mary Queen of Scots.
1607 Fraternal schism in House of Habsburg. Rudolf II withdraws to Prague.	1588 The English fleet destroys the Spanish Armada.
1618 The Defenestration of Prague starts the Thirty Year's War.	
1620 Battle of the White Mountain. Final victory of Counter-Reformation.	
1623 *Foundation of Salzburg University.*	
1648 Peace of Westphalia ends Thirty Year's War.	
1658–1705 Leopold I: all Habsburg domains united.	1665 The Plague in London.
	1669 The Turks conquer Crete.
	1674 Jan Sobieski elected King of Poland.
1677 *Foundation of Innsbruck University.*	
1679 The plague in Vienna: possibly 100,000 victims.	
1683 Second Turkish Siege of Vienna and final disposal of Turkish menace.	
1683 *First Vienna coffee house.* The Graben Column in Vienna commemorates delivery from the plague and from the Turks.	

The chronicle of the House of Habsburg in Austria is not unlike the course of a jet airliner: a relatively steep climb to maximum altitude, followed by a long and gradual decline.

In choosing Rudolf to repair the ravages of the "terrible interregnum" the Diet of Augsburg, while confident that he was strong enough to preserve law and order in the south-east, little realised that it was his ambition and destiny to found a "permanent dynasty". A contemporary account of the first Habsburg describes him as "tall, with long legs, delicately made, with a small head, a pale face and a long nose, little hair, long slim hands: a man temperate in food and drink and other things, a wise and intelligent man". Or as another version has it: "Valiant from his youth on, a man intelligent and powerful but also favoured by fortune, of tall stature with a hooked nose and a grave expression, whose dignity revealed the strength of his character."

His immediate successors expanded and consolidated Rudolf's admirable beginning. First came the acquisition of Carinthia and Carniola, then of some property in what is now Vorarlberg. In 1363, a landmark in Austria history, the House of Habsburg acquired Tyrol; or rather the Countess Margareta Maultasch, a grand-daughter of the great Count Meinhard of Tyrol, made over to Rudolf IV "the land on the Etsch and the Inn valley with Schloss Tirol and all else appertaining thereto". A good deal of legend has grown up around this colourful Countess. There is even an ungalant suggestion that the name "Maultasch" (literally "bag-mouth") was a reference to her features, whereas in reality it comes from Schloss Maultasch near Terlan in South Tyrol. That she was a distinctly headstrong character is shown by her matrimonial record; after throwing her first husband Johann Heinrich of Bohemia out of the house she married her cousin Ludwig of Brandenburg, a Wittelsbach, and was promptly excommunicated for bigamy. And that she was a resourceful leader is shown by the famous story of how when besieged in the castle of Hochosterwitz in Carinthia she extricated herself and the starving garrison by slaughtering the last remaining ox and lowering it over the walls down to the besiegers. Dismayed by this evidence of the garrison's apparently endless resources the besiegers withdrew. Margareta's tempestuous career eventually ended with her death in Vienna in 1369.

As for the Rudolf IV to whom she bequeathed Tyrol, he did not reign long (1358—1365), but in these short seven years he enlarged St. Stephen's and founded the University in Vienna (1365), which is why he is generally known as Rudolf the Founder. And by the time he died he could boast that "all roads and passes leading from Germany into Italy are now under our control".

Friedrich III (1440—1493), whose magnificent tomb is one of the glories of St. Stephen's Cathedral in Vienna, is one of those controversial figures on whom historians fail to agree. Some accuse him of lethargy and indecision, pointing to his passivity in face of the Hungarian invasion that culminated in the Hungarian King Matthias Corvinus capturing Vienna and making it his capital from 1485 until his death in 1490, while Friedrich made his headquarters at Wiener Neustadt — and waited. Others claim — and with some justification — that Friedrich's sole aim was the expansion of Habsburg power and influence and the consolidation of the dynasty. At all events, this baffling, even mysterious mixture of dignity and inertia was responsible, beyond dispute, for an enormous addition to the Habsburg domains by marrying his son Maximilian to Maria of Burgundy, the daughter of Charles the Bold, who had made Burgundy a powerful and flourishing Duchy stretching from what is now Switzerland right up to the North Sea and including the Franche-Comté, Flanders, Brabant, Zeeland, Holland, Friesland and Luxemburg. These vast possessions were to involve Friedrich's successors in endless wars against France, and eventually Burgundy itself had to be ceded to France in 1493, but the other territories remained in Austrian possession. This was the beginning of the long struggle between Austria and France for the hegemony of Europe that lasted until 1756 and was resumed during the Napoleonic era.

Opinions differ again as to whether it is Friedrich III or his son Maximilian who is referred to in the famous Latin hexameter: "Bella gerant alii tu felix Austria nube" ("Let others wage war for a throne — you, happy Austria, marry"). Some say Maximilian, because he arranged even more lucrative marriages than his father did; others interpret it as including a reference to Friedrich's lack of military enterprise and maintain that the lines were written by Matthias Corvinus himself in a moment of bitterness. What tips the scales in favour of Maximilian is the pentameter of the couplet, which is much less frequently quoted: "Nam quae Mars aliis dat tibi regna Venus" ("The lands that others are given by Mars, you receive from Venus") which can be taken as a reference to the fact that Maximilian's marriage was definitely a love-match as well as a dynastic convenience. There are also two alternative Latin versions of the famous motto A. E. I. O. U. which is indelibly associated with Friedrich III and duly appears on his tomb in St. Stephen's Cathedral:

Austriae est imperare orbi universo
(It is for Austria to rule the entire world)
or
Austria erit in orbe ultima
(Austria will outlast all other powers).

Friedrich III had the double distinction of being the first Habsburg to be crowned Holy Roman Emperor in Rome, and the last Emperor to be crowned in Rome.

After the death of Matthias Corvinus, instead of returning to Vienna he retired to Linz, where he lived in comparative seclusion until his death in 1493, leaving the conduct of affairs to his son Maximilian.

Maximilian I (1493—1519) carried on his father's mission of consolidating the power and influence of the House of Habsburg, and even outdid him as a matchmaker. But in every other respect he was as unlike his father as possible. Against the sombre and turbulent background of his times he stands out like "a knight in shining armour", a paragon of chivalry, manliness and nobility. In the aggrandisement of his territories he displayed both energy and diplomacy, his shrewdest move being his decision to make his Imperial Residence at Innsbruck rather than in Vienna. In Friedrich III's reign the chief threat to the Habsburg domains had come from the East: now the chief enemy was France and her various allies in Italy, particularly the waning power of Venice. Quite apart from political and geographical considerations, Innsbruck offered the hunting and mountaineering that were the Emperor's principal diversions. By the end of his reign all the scattered Habsburg domains were re-united, the crown of the Holy Roman Empire was firmly in Habsburg possession, and Habsburg Austria was for the first time a European power to be reckoned with.

Maximilian was born at Wiener Neustadt on 22 March, 1459. It was soon apparent that he had inherited the admirable qualities of his Portuguese mother and his reserved Styrian father. In 1477 came his happy marriage to Maria of Burgundy that assured the eventual acquisition of the vast Burgundian domains including the Netherlands; but Maria died in 1482 before Maximilian succeeded his father in 1493. He was duly crowned Holy Roman Emperor, but at Trent, not in Rome, as the road to Rome was blocked by the Venetians. Not being crowned by the Pope, he fell back on the device of assuming the title of "elected Emperor" as did all other Habsburg Emperors after him. He next applied himself with resolution and foresight to consolidating the dynasty. In 1496 he betrothed his son Philip ("the Handsome") to Juana of Castile and Aragon ("the Mad"), the fruits of the union being a son who as Charles V was to reign over a greater part of the Continent of Europe than any sovereign before or since, plus Spain's newly acquired territories in the New World, notably Mexico and Peru.

Equally far-seeing was the double marriage in 1515 of Maximilian's two grandchildren; Ferdinand to Anna of Bohemia and Hungary, and Marie to the Jagellon King of Bohemia and Hungary, though it was not until after Maximilian's death in 1519 that they came into their inheritance following the death of the Jagellon King at the battle of Mohács against the Turks under Suleiman the Magnificent. 1526 is another most important milestone in Austrian history, for from now on the heart of the Habsburg domains was the union of Austria, Bohemia and Hungary that lasted until the final disintegration in 1918 and was effected just in time to bear the brunt of the Turkish onslaught. In the case of Hungary the inheritance was "de jure" rather than "de facto", as in 1541 the Turks captured Budapest, and it was not for another century and a half that the great Prince Eugene of Savoy drove them out of Hungary in his brilliant campaign of 1716.

But to return to Maximilian, whose conscientious concern for posterity made him acutely aware of the vulnerability of his vast, sprawling territories. The chief danger was France, stung by the Habsburgs' acquisition of Burgundy; and the closing years of Maximilian's reign were spent in almost incessant warfare against the French kings Louis XI and Charles VIII. In Italy Maximilian had little success against the Venetians, but from the French he took Naples and Milan and established the frontier between Tyrol and Italy that lasted until the Treaty of St. Germain in 1919. Italy also provided him with a second wife, Bianca Maria Sforza, whose tomb can be seen in the church of Stams in Tyrol.

All this time, Maximilian's thoughts had characteristically been turning in the direction of his own tomb, and he duly commissioned artists for the colossal mausoleum in the Hofkirche in Innsbruck that was built especially to house it. If today's taste finds such an addiction morbid, Maximilian was at any rate free from the detestable vice of false modesty. "The man," he said, "who makes no memory of himself in his lifetime will enjoy no memory after his death and will be forgotten as soon as the bells cease to toll." Actually, the tomb was not completed until 1582 and Maximilian is not buried in it. He died at Wels in Upper Austria in 1519 on his way from Innsbruck to Vienna and is buried at Wiener Neustadt.

As well as expanding and consolidating his inheritance Maximilian instituted sweeping reforms in the administration and extended the administrative system in force in Tyrol to the rest of the country. He also made the Upper-Austrian salt-mines a Government monopoly, so establishing the "Salzkammergut" which is now one of Europe's most popular tourist attractions.

It was Maximilian who finally led Austria out of the Middle Ages into the splendour of the Renaissance. He has rightly been called "the last of the Knights", but he was also the first of the Humanists. Himself a historian and autobiographer, he was a generous patron of learning and the arts and founded the Vienna Hofkapelle and Boys' Choir as well as what is now the Austrian National Library. As a writer his versatility ranged from treatises on taxation to gardening and warfare, and he was an assiduous collector of medieval poetry and folklore. "Every gift and blessing," says a chronicler, "was apportioned to him: good health up to a ripe age, a fine if not handsome presence, physical strength and dexterity, a memory that retained all he heard, a keen intelligence and exceptional ingenuity: in short a personality to kindle wonderment and devotion."

In the person of Charles V the House of Habsburg, though not yet the House of Austria, the "Casa d'Austria", reached its zenith. Born in 1500 at Ghent in Flanders, he inherited through his grandfather Maximilian the Austrian lands, including the succession to the thrones of Bohemia and Hungary; through his father Burgundy; and through his mother, Juana of Castile and Aragon, the vast Spanish Empire, shortly to be augmented by the subjugation of the Aztecs in Mexico and the Incas in Peru and by the exploits of Cortes and Magellan. It also included all the Netherlands, Sardinia, Sicily and Naples. It was indeed an Empire "on which the sun never set". Charles was brought up in Spain and became its king in 1516. On the death of Maximilian he was elected Holy Roman Emperor and crowned at Aachen in 1520. In the same year he made the valuable acquisition of the Duchy of Württemberg, so completing the link between the scattered Austrian possessions west of Tyrol and forming them into a single unit. From this impregnable position he now embarked on his self-appointed task of stamping out heresy, his first step being to convene the Diet of Worms in 1521 at which Martin Luther was excommunicated. First however he decided on a partition of his vast inheritance and handed over the Austrian lands to his brother Ferdinand, who thus became Ferdinand I of Austria (1521—1564). From now on there were two Habsburg lines, an Austrian and a Spanish, the former becoming extinct on the male side in 1740 and the latter in 1700. During all this time there was the closest friendship and collaboration between the two Empires, notably in containing the expansionist ambitions of the French king. At first it was Spain which had to bear the brunt of the war against the French, and in 1525 Charles inflicted a decisive defeat at Pavia on François I of France, who had been his rival for the Holy Roman Crown and spent the rest of his life thirsting for revenge. With the French threat at least temporarily eliminated Charles spent the next three years in operations against the Turks under Suleiman the Magnificent, operations which some forty years later were to culminate in the annihilation of the Turkish fleet by his illegitimate son Don John of Austria at the Battle of Lepanto in 1571.

But all this military glory seemed to leave Charles cold: what he had really set his heart on was the extermination of heresy, and in this he was thwarted by the obstinate resistance of the Netherlands. Eventually wearying of the futile struggle he summoned the Knights of the Golden Fleece to Brussels in 1556 and announced his abdication. The Spanish Empire went to his son Philip II, and Ferdinand was crowned Holy Roman Emperor in 1558. Meanwhile Charles retired to a monastery in central Spain where he proceeded (according to present-day medical opinion) to eat himself to death. At all events there is little doubt that he was suffering from arterio-sclerosis, and he died in 1558.

Meanwhile Ferdinand, having been delegated by Charles in 1522 to rule the Austrian lands from Alsace to Hungary, duly entered into his Bohemian inheritance in 1526 after the battle of Mohács, but in Hungary the nobles under Janos Zapolya allied themselves with the advancing Turks, who soon overran the whole country. For the next 150 years or more Austria was involved in the same protracted operations against the Turks as Spain was against the French. In 1529 Suleiman the Magnificent at the head of a Turkish army some 30,000 strong actually reached the gates of Vienna. The siege was eventually raised, but the Austrian forces were too numerically inferior to follow up their success and the Turks completed their occupation of

Hungary in 1541 with the capture of Budapest, which remained their headquarters for the next 150 years.

During the second half of the 16th century the rulers of Austria were indeed hard pressed, for as well as the ever-present Turkish menace in the east there was the advance of Protestantism in all its various forms — particularly Lutheranism — from the west and north. Ferdinand, who had been brought up in Spain and was also a devout Catholic, viewed with dismay the immense strides the Protestants were making in Austria, especially among the aristocracy, and after the Religious Peace of Augsburg in 1555 ("cujus regio, ejus religio"), he invited Ignatius Loyola to send some Jesuit teachers to Vienna. So began the Counter-Reformation, yet another landmark in Austrian history.

Ferdinand's son Maximilian II (1564—1576), despite strong personal Protestant leanings, maintained a lukewarm Catholic attitude in the affairs of State and did little or nothing to arrest the Protestant tide. Rudolf II (1576—1612) did even less: a brooding, introspective character, he withdrew altogether from public life and shut himself up in the Citadel in Prague, devoting himself to his superb collection of paintings and manuscripts and the company of astronomers, astrologists and alchemists. Among his closest friends was the great astronomer Johannes Kepler. Small wonder that in 1607 the nobles turned to Rudolf's brother Matthias for a lead. But when Rudolf died and Matthias (1611—1619) became Emperor conditions deteriorated still further: Turkish incursions were almost continuous, and there was no one to give a lead to the Counter-Reformation. The Emperor's final humiliation came when his envoys to Bohemia were unceremoniously bundled out of a window in Prague, and although history has it that they fell soft and came to no harm, the insult could not be ignored. To make matters worse, it was precisely at this juncture that the Emperor Matthias died, but fortunately his successor, Ferdinand II (1619—1637) was a man of sterner stuff altogether. He had been brought up by Jesuits and was as determined to root out heresy in his domains as Philip II was in Spain. Ferdinand took immediate measures to suppress the revolt of the Bohemian nobles, who had declared Bohemia independent of Habsburg domination and had elected as King a Calvinist who knew nothing of the country or of military strategy, the so-called "Winter King".

At the head of an army swollen with contingents from Italy, Spain, the Papal States and the Bavarian League Ferdinand inflicted such a crushing defeat on the Bohemian Protestant nobles at the Battle of the White Mountain in 1620 that the Bohemian aristocracy, and even Bohemian culture, was virtually obliterated for close on two hundred years. The "Winter King" fled from Prague even before the battle started, having allowed time to help himself to some of the Citadel's treasures before departing. And that was the end of the Reformation in Bohemia.

What had started as primarily a religious struggle now flared up into a more or less general war all over Europe and finally resolved itself into an open struggle for the hegemony of Europe between Habsburg Austria and Bourbon France. Any pretensions that the struggle was of a religious nature were rudely dispelled by France's alliance with Protestant Sweden under Gustavus Adolphus. During the welter of private wars that went on for the rest of Ferdinand II's reign most of the fighting took place in Bohemia, where the Austrians bore the brunt of the Swedish southward thrust. Gustavus Adolphus himself was killed at the battle of Lützen in 1632, but still the Swedes came on, until they suffered a more serious check at the Battle of Nördlingen in 1634.

Eleven years later they pushed even further south and after capturing the town of Korneuburg just to the north-east of Vienna were actually within sight of the city before the threat to their long and vulnerable supply lines forced them to withdraw without a fight.

As the Thirty Years' War dragged on there flashed across the scene the scintillating and enigmatic figure of Albert von Wallenstein, Prince of Friedland (1583—1634). He had shown himself a brilliant military commander at an early age and had taken part in Ferdinand's operations against Venice in 1617. He rose rapidly from one command to another and was loaded with honours and estates by his Emperor, but characteristically did not put in an appearance at the Battle of the White Mountain. His energy, and above all his successes, made him many enemies, and in 1630 the Emperor Ferdinand was persuaded at the Diet of Regensburg to dispense with his services, whereupon Wallenstein returned to Prague and busied himself with astrological studies, to which he had been addicted from his earlist youth. It was soon obvious however that he was indispensable to the Emperor's cause: he was recalled and reinstated, raised his own "private" army, and thrashed the Swedes at the Battle of Lützen in 1632 at which Gustavus Adolphus was killed. But now comes the mystery. Instead of following up his victory Wallenstein withdrew to winter quarters in Bohemia. Why? Furthermore, his campaign in the following summer of 1633 was conducted with the utmost lethargy and indecision. The only explanation is that he had already decided to flout the Emperor's orders, which were to beat down heresy by force and exterminate it, ruthlessly and without exception, wherever it was encountered. Wallenstein seems to have persuaded himself that with his brilliant personality he could negotiate with the Swedes for a complete re-organisation of the Empire, with himself as the supreme authority, and with a rather more tolerant religious policy. His proposals were received with suspicion by the Swedes and eventually (and inevitably) came to the ears of the Emperor, who in February 1634 signed an indictment on a charge of high treason and ordered him to be taken alive or dead. Accordingly a murder was arranged and carried out at Cheb in Bohemia. Among those who organised the murder on behalf of the Emperor one regrets to find the names of three Scottish soldiers, or rather colonels, of fortune: Gordon, Butler and Leslie. They were handsomely rewarded.

So it was on this discordant note that Ferdinand II's reign closed three years later. The responsibility for Wallenstein's murder was undoubtedly his, and three hundred years later Wallenstein's preference for negotiation instead of carnage seems more attractive than it did at the time. On the other hand the Emperor too was a strong personality who could brook no disobedience in the execution of his orders to exterminate heresy, no usurpation of his Imperial authority. Gifted with military genius and political vision far ahead of his time, Wallenstein was also cursed with pride, ambition and disloyalty. The verdict of posterity is still open.

Ferdinand III (1637—1657) carried on where his father had left off, having already been given command of the Imperial armies after Wallenstein's murder. After the Swedes had finally withdrawn northwards he managed in 1648 to negotiate the Peace of Westphalia that brought the Thirty Years' War to an end. If on paper the terms seemed not unfavourable, the implications of the Peace were a distinct set-back to Austrian aspirations to the hegemony of Europe. Alsace had to be ceded to France, and the idea of a vast and united Catholic domain under Habsburg leadership as a bulwark against Islam had to be abandoned. Worse still, Austria had from now on to reckon with the constant and implacable hostility of France, who was prepared to ally herself with any power, even the Turks, if it would serve to break Austria. It was indeed fortunate for Austria that during the long turmoil of the Thirty Years' War the Turks made no move, either because of some change of policy in their high command, or because they were fully occupied by their eastward expansion against Persia, or, which was most probable, from a contemptuous indifference to internal Christian quarrels. But the day was to come.

By the time Ferdinand III ended his days in 1657 his domains were once again under firm central administration and the Counter-Reformation had been finally disposed of. Ferdinand was the first of four successive Emperors who were not only skilful musicians and patrons of music but even composers. As well as composing a good deal of church music he also completed an opera for the Jesuits, and in 1653 had the entire Vienna Hofkapelle, complete with all its instruments and properties, shipped up the Danube to the Imperial Diet at Regensburg. His successor Leopold I (1657—1705), the most prolific composer of the four, specialised in "Singspiele" to be sung, acted and danced by members of the Court or even of the Imperial House. In other respects too Leopold was eminently a man of peace, which makes it all the more unfortunate that his long reign was virtually one long war, and on two fronts. That he succeeded in not only preserving, but actually enhancing, the power and prestige of Austria was referred to at the time as the "Mirakel des Hauses Oesterreich". Though no military genius himself he had the knack, unfortunately not vouchsafed to some of the later Habsburgs, of discovering and exploiting talent in others: in other words, he was well-served.

Amid all the marching and counter-marching of the Thirty Years' War Salzburg was an oasis of peace. But it was far from inactive. It was not part of Austria in those days, but an independent territory ruled over by a Prince-Archbishop who wielded temporal as well as spiritual power, as Wolfgang Amadeus Mozart was to find out in 1781. In the year 1587 the incumbent was the redoubtable Wolf Dietrich of Raitenau, who conceived the idea of making cramped, medieval Salzburg into a fine, spacious city, "the Rome of the north". One night, very conveniently for his plan, the magnificent old Romanesque Cathedral was found to be on fire, and surprisingly little effort was made to put the fire out. How it originated will never be known, but the "accident" fitted in remarkably well with Wolf Dietrich's plans. His next step was to build a fine palace for his mistress (or one of them) Salome Alt. Originally it was named Altenau, but Wolf's successor Marcus Sitticus changed it to Myerabela, now Mirabell. Unfortunately almost the whole building was gutted by fire in 1818. Apart from irregularities in his private life, Wolf Dietrich injudiciously involved himself in an unsuccessful war with Bavaria. He was deposed and imprisoned in the Hohensalzburg Fortress, where he died in 1612. There is an Austrian proverb to the effect that what comes after is seldom better: Wolf's successor and nephew Marcus Sitticus indulged in even more flagrant profligacies than his uncle, but only for seven years (1612—1619). It was left to Paris Lodron (1619—1653), probably the greatest of all Salzburg's Prince-Archbishops, to complete the rebuilding of Salzburg. The opening of the new Cathedral in 1628 was a splendid occasion, including a Mass in 53 parts performed by 5 choirs, 5 organs and 3 groups of trumpets and drums.

The feasting and revelry went on for 8 days, but amid all the pomp and circumstance the Archbishop remembered that in the 17th century any sizeable community had to be able to defend itself if it was to survive. It was Paris Lodron who completed the city's defensive fortifications, remnants of which can still be seen on the Kapuzinerberg. Finally, this remarkable prelate also presided over the opening of Salzburg University in 1623.

After the accession of Leopold I in 1657 Austria needed a long period of peace to recover from the exertions and disappointments of the Thirty Years' War. But there was to be little respite; as if the Turkish threat was not enough, Vienna was assailed in 1679 by a scourge more deadly than anything 17th century military commanders could think up — the Plague. The Emperor was obliged to withdraw to Mariazell in Styria, and the total number of victims was estimated at close on 100,000. The city's eventual delivery from its ravages is commemorated by the lovely column in the Graben put up on the orders of the Emperor Leopold.

And then came 1683 and Vienna's supreme hour of trial. Having remained aloof and inactive during the Thirty Years' War the Turks now saw their opportunity. After turning the greater part of Central Europe into a shambles the long wars had left the Powers exhausted and divided; whereas the Turks were at the zenith of their power, with an Empire that stretched from Baghdad to Morocco, and from the Persian Gulf to the Danube; and beyond the Danube Vienna, Prague and the whole of Central Europe beckoned. Moreover they had allies. Their policy of religious toleration made them in Magyar eyes more attractive masters than the Austrians, whose religious intolerance was little if anything short of persecution. Gathering adherents as it rolled north-westwards, a motley but undoubtedly colourful Turkish host over 300,000 strong surged up against Austria's eastern frontier early in 1683 under the command of the Grand Vizier Kara Mustafa.

In acting as a bulwark against the Turks Leopold was in fact left no choice. True, it was Austria's mission in European history to act as the south-eastern support of Latin civilisation against Islam; and some historians have even gone so far as to say that this was the principal justification for the existence of the Austrian Empire at all. But in this year of grace 1683 it was simply and solely a matter of survival. Faced by this vast horde, where was Leopold to look for allies? Many of the waverers had already been detached by the blandishments of Louis XIV of France, who supported the Turks. The Pope made a financial contribution to replenish the almost exhausted Austrian treasury, but the nearest available source of manpower was the sprawling and unstable Kingdom of Poland, and here Leopold did indeed find a friend in need.

Ten years earlier the Turks had thrust northwards and been defeated by a Polish force under Jan Sobieski, who was elected King of Poland in the following year. Jan Sobieski was a giant of a man and a fearless and redoubtable warrior whose language was as flamboyant as his appearance. His opinion of the Turks may be judged from his proclamation on ascending the throne: "It is our intention," he said, "to pursue these barbarians from victory to victory over the very frontiers that belched them forth upon Europe; in a word, not to conquer and curb the monster but to hurl him back into the deserts, to exterminate him, to raise upon his ruins the Empire of Byzantium, this enterprise alone is chivalrous; this alone is noble, wise, decisive."

In this Crusading spirit Jan Sobieski at the head of a Polish army 20,000 strong joined forces with Duke Charles of Lorraine in command of 25,000 Austrians plus sundry small contingents from South German Principalities. Even so Duke Charles was outnumbered by nearly 7 to 1 and a head-on clash was to be avoided at all costs. The two commanders accordingly withdrew to Tulln on the Danube to re-group, the Emperor left Vienna, and the Turks invested it on the east, north and south, thereby setting the pattern for a similar manoeuvre over 250 years later — only in 1945 there was no German relieving army.

Resolute and defiant, Vienna prepared itself for the siege. The whole population helped in constructing ramparts and manning the defences. Even women were conscripted, but even with the addition of civilian volunteers the defenders numbered at most 15,000.

Kara Mustafa soon realised that a direct assault was out of the question, but was perfectly content to bide his time and starve the city out. After two months of attrition and violent artillery duels the garrison, sadly reduced in numbers, was on the point of starvation when the relieving army some 50,000 strong at last set out and made its way through the Vienna Woods to what is now Leopoldsberg, where very early on a September morning the two commanders, Duke Charles and the Polish King, heard Mass in the little chapel and prepared for battle. From his vantage-point near the top of the tower of St. Stephen's Cathedral the intrepid commander of the beleaguered garrison, Count Rüdiger Starhemberg, co-ordinated its operations with those of the relieving force. Kara Mustafa was now caught on two fronts. Duke Charles' men surged into Nussdorf, Heiligenstadt and Grinzing. The armoured Polish cavalry were more than a match for the Turkish horsemen and before the day was out the Turks were fleeing eastwards in a disorderly rabble, abandoning their lines to be plundered by the victors. One particularly valuable prize was an enormous golden crescent, which was duly placed at the very top of the spire of St. Stephen's Cathedral as a symbol of victory.

All Europe breathed a sigh of relief, and congratulations poured in from every Court in Europe. Only in Vienna was there no public rejoicing or revelry — the people had lost and suffered too much. The rout of the Turks was the beginning of the long decline of the Ottoman (Turkish) Empire which, like the Austrian, finally disintegrated at the end of World War I. For the House of Habsburg it was its finest hour, the zenith of its power and prestige, "maximum altitude"; and the decline was not yet.

One final feature of this *annus mirabilis:* it was towards the end of the year that the first coffee-house opened in Vienna.

CHAPTER THREE

The "Baroque Emperors" and Prince Eugene

Austria	Elsewhere
1656–1723 *Baroque architect J. B. Fischer v. Erlach (father).*	
1658–1705 Leopold I.	
1660–1723 *Baroque architect Jakob Prandtauer of Tyrol.*	
1686 Recapture of Budapest.	
	1688 Deposition of the last of the Stuart Kings of England.
1695 *Work started on Schönbrunn Palace (first plan).*	
1697–1717 Prince Eugene's campaigns against the Turks.	
1699 Peace of Carlowitz.	
	1700 Spanish Habsburg line becomes extinct in the male line.
1701 The "Grand Alliance" of Austria, England and Holland.	
1701–14 War of Spanish Succession. (Prince Eugene and the Duke of Marlborough).	
1704 Battle of Blenheim.	
1705–11 Joseph I.	
	1707 Union of England and Scotland.
	1709 Russian victory over the Swedes at Poltawa.
1711–40 Karl VI.	
1713 The Pragmatic Sanction. Peace of Utrecht.	
1714 Treaty of Rastatt.	1714–27 George I of England, the first of the House of Hanover.
1718 Peace of Passarowitz.	
1721 *Completion of the Vienna Belvedere, Summer Palace of Prince Eugene of Savoy.*	

It is one of the supreme ironies of Austrian history that Leopold I, who was essentially a man of peace and a munificent patron of the arts, should have spent practically the whole of his long reign in continuous warfare, and on two fronts. Of the four "baroque" emperors from Ferdinand III to Karl VI he is perhaps the greatest, if not the greatest of all the old Habsburg dynasty before it became the House of Habsburg-Lorraine in 1740. One attribute in particular sets him apart, and above his contemporaries, the flair for knowing when to control or intervene in person, and when to delegate or even to let matters take their course. Moreover he was an excellent judge of his fellow-men and knew how to get the best out of those who served

43

him. There was an inner poise in his nature that precluded anything ill-considered or impetuous: no important step was taken without the most careful deliberation, but deliberation was never an excuse for vacillation or indecision. Nor did he show any desire for the limelight: he was perfectly prepared for his lieutenants to bask in it if they had deserved it. At his death the House of Habsburg was still at "maximum altitude"; as well as being the undisputed master of Central and south-eastern Europe it had earned the gratitude and dispelled the apprehensions of the western world, and on the eastern front had gone over to the offensive against the Turks.

Whatever Leopold's stature as an Emperor, there can be no two opinions about his stature as a patron of the arts. As a practising musician and a composer he was the most prolific, if not the most naturally gifted, of the four "baroque" Emperors, and he is known to have composed at least 155 unison and part-songs, not to mention close on 80 sacred works, 17 ballets, and 9 "feste trionfali", dramatic performances with music, something like pageants. His successor Joseph I was more naturally gifted, but did not live long enough to make his mark as a composer, or for that matter as a ruler. His early death after a reign of only 6 years, as well as extinguishing the high hopes that had been reposed in him, very nearly had disastrous consequences for the dynasty. In 1700 the male line of the Spanish Habsburgs had died out, and Leopold had therefore decreed that his elder son Joseph should rule the Austrian territories and be crowned Holy Roman Emperor, and that his younger son Karl should be King of Spain. Joseph's untimely death therefore meant that there was every possibility of the two crowns being united, with fatal consequences to the balance of power in Europe. One direct result of Joseph's death was England's withdrawal from Austria's side in the War of the Spanish Succession, as will be seen in due course.

The last of the "baroque" Emperors, and the last of the "old" Habsburgs, Karl VI, was therefore handicapped from the start by unexpectedly becoming the ruler of Austria instead of succeeding to the Spanish throne for which he had been trained. At heart, he remained "Spanish" all his life, and introduced the elaborate Spanish ceremonial into the Vienna Court, one survival of which is the famous "Spanish" Riding-School in Vienna. He too was an excellent composer and violinist and epitomised the full flowering of Austrian baroque, notably the "Charles" Church (Karlskirche) in Vienna. Yet for the whole of his reign he was haunted by the dread of the male line dying out as in Spain, and within two years of his accession he introduced the "Pragmatic Sanction" (1713), a family statute which proclaimed the indivisibility of all Habsburg lands and made provision for their being ruled by a woman in the event of the male line becoming extinct (he had no male heir). In view of the generally accepted Salic Law, such a provision required the approval of the chief European powers. Not a strong bargaining position for Karl. The English Government was quick to appreciate the possibilities, and demanded (and obtained) the closing down of the Austrian East India Trading Company at Ostend. The French drove an even harder bargain, the reversion to the Duchy of Lorraine.

But this is to anticipate. There is first the matter of Austria's long wars on two fronts — against the Turks and against the French.

There have been all too frequent occasions in Austrian history where a resounding victory has not been followed up and the opportunity has been lost. Such was certainly not the case in 1683. The army that had relieved Vienna kept hard on the heels of the retreating Turks all down through Hungary, and among the Archduke Charles' cavalry officers was a young Prince, and a foreigner at that, who was to become Austria's greatest military commander,

Prince Eugene of Savoy. How did he come to be there at all?

In Paris, on 18 October 1663, to Eugene Maurice Count of Soissons, of the House of Savoy-Carignan, a French general and "prince of the blood", i. e. a scion of the royal House of Bourbon, there was born a son who was destined to exert a decisive influence on Austrian history: Prince Eugene of Savoy. His mother was Olympia Mancini, a niece of the all-powerful Cardinal Mazarin. On his father's side the child Eugene was descended from the House of Savoy, Bourbon and Habsburg, and on his mother's from an upper-middle-class Roman family. French by birth, he was of predominantly Italian descent.

His early years gave little promise of an outstanding future. On the premature death of his father his mother, a woman of beauty and ambition, set her cap at Louis XIV, "Le Roi Soleil", and became involved in desperate rivalries with younger aspirants that left her little time for the education of her children. Eventually implicated in a particularly scandalous poisoning affair she was obliged to make a dash for the Netherlands frontier and never again set foot on French soil. The children were brought up by their grandmother and an ill-tempered aunt but were given no proper education; nor did Eugene himself, for the time being at any rate, succeed in rising above his dismal environment, living on the charity of Savoy relatives. Moreover he was of a far from prepossessing outward appearance, short and sickly, so that it was hardly surprising that the proud and ceremonious Louis XIV contemptuously disowned this particular member of the family.

Despite his frequently proclaimed preference for his father's profession Eugene was to be fobbed off with the Church, and it was on the rejection of one of his many applications to join the army that in 1683 he took leave of France in the company of Prince Conti, the King's son-in-law, to seek his fortune in the service of the Austrian Emperor. There was no inkling in France of the consequences this step was to entail. After taking part as a cavalry volunteer in the raising of the Turkish siege of Vienna in the same year Eugene was soon rising rapidly in the Emperor's service. Before the year was out he was commanding a regiment of dragoons, and particularly distinguished himself during Archduke Charles' brilliant reconquest of Hungary, culminating in the re-capture of Budapest in 1686 after it had been in Turkish hands for 150 years. After a spell in the West in command of an independent Imperial force in support of the Duke of Savoy in his struggle against France he was promoted to the rank of Acting Field-Marshal and returned to the East, where in 1697 he was given the supreme command against the Turks on the recommendation of Rüdiger von Starhemberg, the defender of Vienna in 1683, who particularly extolled his "generous and impartial demeanour".

It was against the Turks that Prince Eugene achieved his most dazzling successes, notwithstanding all the glories of his later campaigns at the side of the Duke of Marlborough. And it was his decisive victory at Zenta that led up to the Peace of Carlowitz in 1699, by which Austria not only secured the whole of Hungary but also acquired Croatia, Slavonia and the lovely land of Transylvania further south-east.

Meanwhile, in the west the War of the Spanish Succession (1701—1714) had broken out, the Spanish throne having become vacant on the death of the last Spanish Habsburg in the male line. Austria and Louis XIV of France, each with candidates of their own, both had their eyes on the glittering prize — Spain, Naples, Sicily, Sardinia, Lombardy, Belgium, Spanish America, the Philippines and scattered territories on the African continent. In 1701 the Emperor Leopold astutely formed the "Grand

Alliance" of Austria, England and Holland, and all was set for a supreme trial of strength for the hegemony of Europe. In 1702, by a brilliant forced march across the mountains that had never before been ventured, Prince Eugene eluded the French army lying in wait for him in the Verona gap, and eventually joined forces with the English commander, the Duke of Marlborough. In the critical situation brought about by Bavaria siding with France in 1703 and by the Hungarian uprising under Ferenc Rakoczy in the same year Eugene finally succeeded in overcoming opposition to his appointment as President of the Imperial War Council. In the following year he shared in Marlborough's decisive victory at Blenheim which altered the entire course of the war, and the whole of Bavaria passed into Austrian possession. In 1706 came Eugene's victory near Turin that drove the French out of the whole of northern Italy, and Marlborough's victory at Ramilies that led to the capture of Brussels. There followed in 1708 and 1709 the two hard-won victories, again at Marlborough's side, of Oudenarde and Malplaquet, which secured the Spanish Netherlands.

This brilliant run of success was brought to an abrupt end by the events of 1711: the Emperor Joseph died, and there was a change of Government in England. Fearing the possibility of a union of all the Austrian and Spanish domains under a single crown, and its overwhelming effect on the European balance of power, England withdrew from the war, and in 1713 both England and Holland made a separate peace with France by the Treaty of Utrecht. It was the first time in history that England, a predominantly naval power, had played such a brilliant part in a general war on land, and her defection meant that all Eugene's and Marlborough's victories during the last ten years were to all intents and purposes nullified. For the Emperor Karl the war was irretrievably lost, and in 1714 he concluded with France the Treaty of Rastatt, by which

The Emperor Maximilian I, by Albrecht Dürer

Prince Eugene of Savoy

Spain and all the overseas territories fell to a Bourbon Prince. All the Emperor managed to get was Naples, Lombardy, Sardinia and Belgium, all somewhat of a "white elephant" in view of their remoteness from the Habsburg crownlands and their vulnerability to French attack. And poor compensation for the dashing of his Spanish hopes.

It was not long before Prince Eugene was back on the Eastern front, where there was plenty for him to do. In 1717 he captured Belgrade from the Turks, and in 1718 the Peace of Passarowitz gave large areas of present-day Serbia and Rumania to Austria, including Belgrade itself. No doubt the Empire was becoming dangerously over-stretched, but the importance of Prince Eugene's campaigns was that they consolidated the Danube frontier and secured control of Hungary (territorially).

Prince Eugene's military power was later rivalled by his unremitting activities as a statesman. His position as Chairman of the Imperial War Council was tantamount to that of Prime Minister. During the reigns of Joseph I and Karl VI he became more and more involved in high-level politics and in 1712 undertook a mission to London to persuade the new English Government not to withdraw from the war: the mission brought him high honours but no success. One of his greatest diplomatic successes was in the negotiations leading up to the Treaty of Rastatt in 1714, whereby he secured far better terms than the actual military situation warranted. In reward for these services he was appointed Governor-General (Statthalter) of two of the most important territories accruing to Austria from the former Spanish domains, Lombardy and the Netherlands. After the final defeat of the Turks his position was unchallenged, and his contemporaries regarded him as "the Emperor behind the scenes".

In actual fact however this dazzling public image was not reflected by reality. The Emperor Karl VI always reserved final decisions to himself, and the alien Prince never quite succeeded in finding a sure foothold amid the maze of intrigue at the Vienna Court. In 1725, as a result of attacks by his representative in the Netherlands, the Marquis de Prie, he was obliged to lay down his office of Statthalter. At the same time his influence on foreign policy gradually increased, and by manipulating his own personal system of secret diplomacy he succeeded in outmanoeuvring the official architect of Austrian foreign policy, Graf Sinzendorf. The Emperor's principal ambassadors addressed their secret reports direct to Eugene, from whom they also took advice and instructions. With only one secretary Eugene carried on all this vast correspondence with his own hand, and made his reports to the Emperor alone. Through his hands passed a stream of gold from the Imperial coffers for the bribery of foreign agents and the acquisition of confidential information. And for the time being the Prince's highly personal system of diplomacy, which was by no means over-particular in the methods it employed, certainly bore fruit: alliances were concluded with Russia and Prussia, and in 1731 England and France agreed to recognise the "Pragmatic Sanction" providing for Maria Theresia's eventual accession to the Habsburg inheritance, but at a stiff price.

His influence on internal affairs on the other hand, apart from military matters, never amounted to very much. As an alien he deliberately abstained from taking any part in drawing up the Pragmatic Sanction, an issue that affected the entire Habsburg domains. While constantly campaigning for modernisation and centralisation he never initiated any reforms himself. As a statesman, for all his intermittent flashes of subtlety and finesse, he never matched the elan and audacity of his military exploits. In the last years of his life, from 1732 to 1736, increasing senility reduced him to a shadow of his former self. The Emperor was lending his ear to new counsellors now, and Eugene was almost imperceptibly eased off the scene. If therefore the reverses that were suffered during the War of the Polish Succession cannot be laid at his door, there is still an element of tragedy about the last years of this great commander and statesman. In the words of King Frederick of Prussia, Eugene outlived his own renown. He died in his Belvedere Palace in Vienna in 1736, and as Maria Theresia observed some years later, with his death Fortune seemed to have turned her back on the House of Austria. He is buried in St. Stephen's Cathedral in Vienna.

Posterity also remembers Eugene as a great collector and patron of the arts. Although the Empire he served has long since disintegrated his palaces, his summer (Belvedere) and winter residences in Vienne, Schlosshof on the March-feld plain to the east of the capital, and a number of residences in Hungary are still standing. As a reward for his victories in Hungary the Emperor presented him with vast estates in that country, and there were also the princely salaries that went with his official position as Statthalter as well as financial rewards from friendly foreign powers, not to mention the unfailing munificence of his Imperial masters. From all these resources the Prince, whose personal needs were modest without a family to support, was able to devote vast sums to the realisation of his aspirations in the realms of Art and Learning. The Vienna Belvedere attests not only the skill of its architect Lukas von Hilde-brandt but also the good taste and breadth of vision of the Prince who commissioned it.

A confirmed bachelor, Eugene's personality has not come down to posterity with distinctive clarity. The thousands of extant letters from him on political and military matters contain hardly a single observation of a personal nature. In his personal relationships he was reserved, even with-drawn, but eminently likeable. What is certain is that apart from one or two defects of character, such as vindictiveness, relentless animosity towards his enemies, and a definite penchant for intrigue, he must have possessed a number of outstanding human qualities, sufficient to ensure the love and admiration of his contemporaries despite his unprepossessing outward appearance.

Though an alien Prince he rendered Austria more devoted and distinguished service than any other military commander in its long history, the ideal for which he strove being a supra-national Central Europe from the frontiers of France to the Adriatic and the Balkans under the Crown of the Holy Roman Empire worn by a Habsburg. Of the three Emperors he served he himself is said to have remarked: "Leopold I was my father, Joseph I my brother, and Karl VI my master."

Alas — Maria Theresia's observation was only too well-founded. Barely two years after Prince Eugene's death much of the Balkan territory acquired during his brilliant campaign of 1716-18 was lost as the result of yet another war against the Turks. In alliance with Russia Austria suffered a series of reverses, and by the Treaty of Belgrade in 1739 had to give up nearly all the outlying territories acquired by the Treaty of Passarowitz 21 years before. What was worse, she lost a great deal of political prestige, and Balkan hopes turned to the emergent power of Russia. In the West too things did not go well for Austria, and the War of the Polish Succession (1733—1738), during which the aged Prince Eugene was in command of the Emperor's forces for the last time, ended in the Peace of Vienna in 1738, by which Austria had to cede Naples and Sicily to the new Bourbon King of Spain, and was awarded Parma and Piacenza in compensation. In another exchange, the Duchy of Lorraine was to go to France on the death of its present ruler, Duke Franz Stephan, who two years previously had married the young heir to the Austrian throne, the Archduchess Maria Theresia. In compensation for the loss of Lorraine, Austria acquired the Grand Duchy of Tuscany.

Notwithstanding these military reverses the Vienna Court now rivalled its French counterpart at Versailles as the centre of European cultural life. After the great victory, instead of remaining aloof in Olympian grandeur and haughtily accepting the gratitude and homage of Central European princelings, Vienna opened her arms to everything Europe had to offer. Artists and craftsmen, scholars and scientists from Italy, Spain, the Netherlands, even France came flocking to participate in, or simply to watch the pageant of the "Mirakel des Hauses Oesterreich". The general feeling of relief at deliverance from almost a century of war and pestilence erupted in a great upsurge of creative activity, in literature and music but above all in architecture. At the crossroads of Europe, Vienna became the great melting-pot in which the art and culture of the Roman south, the Slav east and the Germanic north crystallised out into Baroque, or rather Austrian Baroque.

Baroque is still part and parcel of Austrian life, as well as the outstanding feature of the Austrian landscape. Baroque is more than a form of art; it is a way of life, based on compromise and an appeal to the senses. Though architecture and ceremonial are its principal manifestations, it came in time to permeate even the humblest objects and occupations. Briefly, Baroque is the outward and visible sign of inward and spiritual emotion, the manifestation in pomp and pageantry of confidence in the future and delight in the present. It is an attempt to make the mysteries of religion comprehensible to the ordinary citizen by representing them in a colourful and decorative form that makes its appeal to the senses rather than to the intelligence. Baroque architecture is above all the art of the façade, of presenting a decorative and immediately impressive exterior. It is also the epitome of the Counter-Reformation: no more Gothic austerity, let there be light, frivolity and exuberance. Baroque is flamboyant, elegant, and above all triumphant, but never ostentatious. And at the centre of many a welter of saints and angels in a Baroque mural or fresco there will be the Emperor, in the sort of apotheosis that can be seen in the Austrian National Library in Vienna.

One superb example of Baroque architecture in Austria is Melk on the Danube. Others that come to mind are Salzburg Cathedral (very early Baroque); the Belvedere, Schönbrunn Palace and the Holy Trinity Column in the Graben, all in Vienna; and the Monastery of St. Florian in Upper Austria. But the supreme architectural symbol of Baroque is the Karlskirche in Vienna, with its great green copper dome and the two pillars in imitation of Trajan's column in Rome, epitomising the union of Roman power and Christianity. Three of the great Baroque builders whose names crop up at almost every turn all over Austria were Johann Bernhard Fischer von Erlach (1656—1723), whose principal monuments are the Karlskirche in Vienna and the Collegiate Church at Salzburg; Johann Lukas von Hildebrandt (1668—1745) who built the Upper and Lower Belvedere for Prince Eugene and the Imperial Chancellery in the Ballhausplatz, both in Vienna; and Jakob Prandtauer (1660—1726), a native of Tyrol, who is assured of immortality for the two great monasteries of Melk on the Danube and St. Florian near Linz in Upper Austria.

The death of the Emperor Karl VI meant more than the end of the Habsburg male line; it was the beginning of the end of Austria's "maximum altitude". With the succession passing through the female line to the House of Habsburg-Lorraine there is the 40 years' splendour of Maria Theresia's reign, and then begins the long, long decline that led to 1918. But for a moment, in this year of grace 1740, Austria is still, outwardly at any rate, at the zenith of her power and prosperity; victorious, happy and glorious. The Counter-Reformation is triumphant everywhere, and Bohemian resistance has been crushed. In the east the Turks have been rolled back to where they started from, and in the west Austria has the support of the two Protestant

54

maritime powers, England and Holland, against France. But behind the glittering façade things are not quite so stable as they seem. Geographically Vienna is now at the centre of all her domains instead of being an outpost on the extreme eastern rim of Western civilisation, but on the other hand the Empire is dangerously over-stretched. Internally too the Empire lacks a firm structure. It is based on allegiance to a family as a result of dynastic marriages; there are no common customs or language, and religious unity is being imposed by force.

Above all, the basis of consent is lacking, in that the Empire is not an association of self-governing States. Yet somehow, for almost another 200 years the dynasty held together a conglomeration of many widely differing and excitable peoples. The Magyars, with their alien customs and their incomprehensible language, were particularly indigestible. How was the ruling House to assimilate their feudal, semi-oriental society, due perhaps to their long association with the Turks? Yet the Magyars were only one of several seemingly incompatible juxtapositions within these vastly distended domains. The small Duchy at the extreme south-east of Western Europe had swollen into a sprawling Empire stretching from the North Sea to the Mediterranean and far down into the Balkans: all present-day Austria (including South Tyrol but not Salzburg), Hungary, Bohemia and Moravia; Silesia; Transylvania; Croatia; Slavonia; Dalmatia; Istria, with Fiume und Trieste; parts of south-west Germany; Belgium; Lombardy; Tuscany; Sardinia; Piacenza and Parma.

It was this vast inheritance that Maria Theresia entered upon in 1740 at the age of 23 with her Consort Franz Stephan of Lorraine. It is still high noon in the Habsburg firmament, but on the far horizon are two small clouds, as yet "no bigger than a man's hand": Russia and Prussia.

CHAPTER FOUR

Maria Theresia and Joseph II

Austria

1740–80 Maria Theresia.
1741–48 War of the Austrian Succession.
1744–50 *Schönbrunn Palace.*

1748 Peace of Aix-la-Chapelle.

1753–92 Prince Kaunitz Imperial Chancellor.
1756 Franco-Austrian defensive alliance.
1756 *Birth of Wolfgang Amadeus Mozart.*
1756–63 The Seven Years' War, ending in the Treaty of Hubertusburg.

1762 *Mozart plays for Maria Theresia at Schönbrunn.*

1765 Death of Franz Stephan of Lorraine. Maria Theresia's son Joseph as co-Regent.
1766 *The Vienna Prater opened to the public.*

Elsewhere

1721–64 Madame de Pompadour.
1740–86 Frederick II (the Great) of Prussia.
1742 *First performance of Händel's "Messiah" in Dublin.*

1745 Failure of "Bonny Prince Charlie's" rising in Scotland.
1749 *Birth of Johann Wolfgang Goethe in Frankfurt.*

1750 *Death of J. S. Bach.*

1757 The victory of Plassey opens India to England.
1762 Death of Elisabeth of Russia.
1762–96 Catherine the Great of Russia.
1763 England acquires Canada by the Peace of Paris.

1770 Captain Cook's voyage to Australia.

Austria	*Elsewhere*
	1770 Marriage of Louis XVI of France and Marie Antoinette, daughter of Maria Theresia.
1772 First Partition of Poland: Austria acquires Galicia.	
1775 *The Gloriette at Schönbrunn.*	
1776 *Founding of the Burgtheater.*	1776 American Declaration of Independence.
1778–79 War of the Bavarian Sucession.	
1780–90 Joseph II.	
1781 *Mozart settles in Vienna.*	
1782 Pope Pius VI visits Vienna.	
1784 *The first General Hospital in Vienna.*	
	1789 Outbreak of the French Revolution.
1790 *Joseph Haydn settles in Vienna on the death of Prince Esterházy.*	1789–97 George Washington first President of the United States.

Storm-clouds usually gather rapidly in Central Europe. Barely had Maria Theresia ascended her throne as Queen of Hungary than they burst upon her. On her northern frontier was a new king with boundless ambitions and no scruples, Frederick II of Prussia, sometimes referred to as Frederick "the Great", although his neighbours probably used a rather different word. He spent most of his reign of 46 years making war on three women: Maria Theresia of Austria, whom he called "the apostolic hag"; Elisabeth of Russia, whom he called "the wild-cat of the north"; and Louis XV of France's Madame de Pompadour, whom he contemptuously dismissed as "Mademoiselle Poisson" on the grounds that her mother had been a fish-wife.

No wonder that the lands to his south seemed to Frederick easy game. A new Queen, very young and very in-experienced, with a Consort who was at first far from popular, found (as she herself put it) a treasury drained by the almost perpetual wars of the last sixty years or so, an army exhausted and in disarray, and advisors who had no counsel to offer. Her position was one of appalling insecurity, and it was precisely at this juncture that without either warning or pretext Frederick marched his soldiers into Austria's rich industrial province of Silesia and in 1741 captured its capital, Breslau, before appreciable Austrian resistance could be organised. It was a blow Maria Theresia never forgot and never forgave. From now on it was to be war to the death with "this robber of Silesia", this "evil man", this "monster", this "ugly neighbour", the "hermit of Sans Souci", until Silesia was recovered. But it never was. The war that started in 1740 dragged on with brief interruptions until 1763. Taking adavantage of Maria Theresia's involvement with Frederick the French, at the head of a general coalition of Powers anxious for a share in the expected spoils, advanced upon Austria and captured Prague. In this year 1741 Austrian fortunes were at their lowest ebb, and Prince Eugene's dying injunction, to put more trust in a strong army and less in the Pragmatic Sanction, was being terribly vindicated. In this dark hour the comparison between the young Queen and Queen Elizabeth I of England is striking: in 1586, when the threat of the Spanisch Armada was looming larger and larger, Elizabeth had rallied her subjects with words that have become immortal: ... "I know I have the body of a weak and feeble woman, but I have the heart and stomach of a King, and think foul scorn that any Prince of Europe should dare to invade the borders of my realm ..."

So now Maria Theresia kindled the loyalty of her Hungarian subjects at her coronation at Pressburg (Bratislava) and within a year had completely turned the tables by driving the French out of Prague and forcing Frederick out of the war — but not out of Silesia. By the Treaty of Aix-la-Chapelle in 1748 Maria Theresia secured recognition (for what it was worth) of the Pragmatic Sanction, but had to acquiesce in Silesia being annexed to Prussia.

Frederick had certainly conducted a campaign of Prussian ruthlessness and efficiency. Dispensing with the formality of a pretext, he had struck with no more justification than (to quote his own words) "an army at readiness, a well-filled Treasury, and a determination to make myself talked about". His attack on Austria was a flagrant violation of the Pragmatic Sanction which Prussia had recognised, but Frederick had as little compunction in tearing up a "srcap of paper" as a later German Emperor had in 1914. And through all the vicissitudes of the two Silesian Wars and the war of the Austrian Succession (1741—1748) he somehow managed to cling on to his ill-gotten gains against all comers. Quite apart from his loathsome medical history, Frederick II does not emerge as a very estimable character. Even George II of England, himself a German, referred to him as "a mischievous rascal, a bad friend, a bad ally, a bad relation and a bad neighbour; in fact, the most dangerous and ill-disposed Prince in Europe". But he was a military genius.

The Treaty of Aix-la-Chapelle settled nothing. With Maria Theresia it was the rape of Silesia that rankled even more than the emergence of a second German power, though for the time being there was no question of a struggle between them for the hegemony of German-speaking Europe. For Maria Theresia it was a question first and foremost of survival, and then of recovering Silesia. After her early military reverses had been to some extent made good, thanks to the Hungarians, she set about putting her diplomatic house in order. The first question that had to be considered was the alliance with England against France. What had Austria really got out of it? And in trying to weaken France, was Austria not playing into the hands of the upstart Prussians?

Austria's delegate at the Peace Conference at Aix-la-Chapelle had been Graf Wenzel Kaunitz (1711—1794). In 1753 Maria Theresia appointed him "Imperial Chancellor" in Vienna, a new post which carried with it full responsibility for all foreign affairs and for all matters pertaining to the Imperial House: the equivalent of Prime Minister, Foreign Secretary and Home Secretary rolled into one. This was a particularly shrewd appointment in view of the fact that Kaunitz' foreign policy was based on mistrust of England and on a detestation of Prussia that amounted to an obsession. "Prussia must be overthrown," he used to reiterate, "if the House of Austria is to survive." After years of patient and tortuous diplomacy Kaunitz eventually succeeded in 1756 in negotiating a defensive Franco-Austrian alliance, as well as an alliance with Russia to complete the encirclement of Prussia. Frederick's reply was to unleash the Seven Years' War (1756—1763) with as little compunction as he had shown over Silesia, his opening move being to invade the peaceful neighbouring State of Saxony, seize its capital, Dresden, confiscate its Treasury, and incorporate its army (by force if necessary) into his own. During the next seven years both sides could claim local but far from bloodless victories, notably the Austrian victory at Kolin (1757) and the dazzling Prussian triumph at Leuthen in the same year. The vast numerical superiority of the Austrians and their allies was counterbalanced by the brilliance of Frederick's generalship and the tenacity of his soldiers. What cost Austria final victory was her failure to follow up the successful Russian invasion of Brandenburg (on one occasion the Russians got as far as Berlin) by opening up a "second front". In the end both sides were willing to settle for a draw. By the Treaty of Hubertusburg in 1763 Austria was forced to say good-bye to all hopes of ever recovering Silesia, but on the other hand her prestige as the leader of a European Coalition stood a good deal higher than before. Yet from Maria Theresia's point of view, even more unpalatable than the loss of Silesia was the revelation that the new power of Prussia now enjoyed the undisputed hegemony of northern

Europe; and the Seven Years' War was only the opening round in a long struggle for supremacy between Austria and Prussia, Habsburg and Hohenzollern, that was to last until the Prussian victory over Austria in 1866 and the proclamation of the German Empire in 1871.

After the Seven Years' War Maria Theresia concentrated on consolidation in the Danube area and the security of her possessions in Italy. Only once did relations with Prussia flare up again into war, the War of the Bavarian Succession (1778-79) in which Austria secured territories along the lower reaches of the River Inn, so fixing the frontier (as it is today) between Upper Austria and Bavaria. The Treaty of Teschen which ended the war was described by Maria Theresia to her Chancellor Kaunitz as "certainly not your most glorious, but definitely your most laborious and expedient achievement in the service of the Monarchy".

Kaunitz was certainly one of the outstanding statesmen of the age. His alliance with France in 1756 reversed an alignment that had become almost a European tradition, one of its consequences being that England automatically veered to the side of Prussia in accordance with her traditional policy of maintaining a balance of power in Europe. Not that England made much contribution to the fighting in Europe — India and Canada were more attractive prizes and the American colonies were growing restive. And at first French assistance to Austria was limited to money for the purchase of help from Russia. In return, France was to expect the cession of the Austrian Netherlands (Belgium) once Frederick and his Prussians had been eliminated. Kaunitz' great tour-de-force was in getting this agreement expanded only a year later into a full-scale military alliance, and in actually persuading France to wage war for six years in defiance of her own interests and simply to prevent the emergence of a second German-speaking power in Europe, whereas in point of fact a moderately strong

61

Prussia represented the one chance of French hegemony in Europe. Even more dazzling was Kaunitz's achievement in talking Russia into fighting for interests that were purely Austrian, adroitly playing on Catherine's personal detestation of Frederick. In the end it was Austria's strategic ineptitude and war-weariness, not her faulty diplomacy, that enabled Frederick to get out of the trap alive.

The death of Maria Theresia's husband Franz Stephan of Lorraine in 1765, and the elevation of her son Joseph to be co-Regent, changed everything. Before the year was out Joseph and Kaunitz were at loggerheads, the Emperor taking exception to the Imperial Chancellor's "private army" in the Imperial Chancellery in the Ballhausplatz. There is no doubt that Kaunitz did have his own methods of keeping the Court plied with information, and had recruited his own staff to carry them out; but he claimed that he was justified by results. In a report to the Emperor not conspicuously lacking in self-adulation he extolled "the incomparable organisation at the Ballhausplatz: few sovereigns can ever have enjoyed such plentiful and accurate information". He eventually succeeded in appeasing the Imperial displeasure and it was not until 1792, two years before his death and two years after Joseph's, that he was finally relieved of his office.

Between 1765, when he became co-Regent, and the death of Maria Theresia in 1780, Joseph asserted himself more and more in the domain of foreign affairs, his principal exploit being a share in the First Partition of Poland in 1772. Though it brought Austria the extensive new Province of Galicia, it was an episode of which Maria Theresia was deeply ashamed for the rest of her life. It was an action that is hard to defend, based purely on expediency and on preserving the balance of power vis-à-vis Russia and Prussia. If these two helped themselves to large slices of Poland, Austria had to do likewise: it was a case of keeping up with the neighbours.

In the later part of Maria Theresia's life there is much that recalls Queen Victoria of England: the large family (Maria Theresia had 16 children, 10 of whom survived her, including Marie-Antoinette who married King Louis XVI of France); the Consort who was never popular with the people as a whole and died long before the Queen; the blend of determination and femininity; the insistence on duty, conscience and morality; and at the end the love and respect of her subjects. And as in the case of Queen Victoria, who at the age of twelve had promised "to be good", goodness was one of Maria Theresia's outstanding attributes. Another quality common to them both was sincerity, without which even the strongest personality makes little impact. It was in the nature of things that Maria Theresia should from the very beginning be the central pivot around which the whole Imperial machine revolved. She had to remain firm, and she had to be resolute in defending her inheritance against marauders looking for an easy kill.

And what in fact did her inheritance amount to? Maria Theresia was very soon faced with the realisation that it was a collection of wholly uncoordinated territories with no unified administration, religion or language. One of her first steps therefore was to set up a supreme Council of State to coordinate all the local Diets. Instead of a vague loyalty to the House of Habsburg-Lorraine there was to be a stable central administration. What had been conspicuously lacking in her father's day were a firm administrative structure, and a basis of "consent" among his multi-racial subjects, as opposed to imposition by force. It was in pursuance of "consent" that she made her dramatic appeal to the Hungarians during her coronation at Pressburg. As regards administrative reform, the hour produced the man, Graf Friedrich Haugwitz (1702—1765), of whom Maria Theresia said later that "Providence sent him in my hour of need". It was Haugwitz who put into practice Maria Theresia's far-reaching administrative and financial reforms, including a new legal code and the complete separation of the law from the executive. Gradually and prudently a new administrative structure was built up by adapting ancient institutions to modern needs. Among the many institutions of Maria Theresia's that are still going strong are the Officers' Military Academy at Wiener Neustadt and the "Theresianum" Diplomatic College in Vienna.

Only in one direction did Maria Theresia show irresolution: she made no attempt to effect changes in the social structure of Hungary, perhaps because as things were she was confident of being able to count on the loyalty of the aristocracy anyway. It was an omission that was to have far-reaching consequences 100 years later.

Maria Theresia's death in 1780 was the end of an era, an era that has been so brilliantly recaptured in Hugo von Hofmannsthal's libretto to the opera "Der Rosenkavalier". It is an era that has a splendid monument in the apartments and gardens of Schönbrunn Palace, Maria Theresia's favourite residence, notably the room in which Wolfgang Amadeus Mozart, aged six, was presented to the Empress by his proud father and immediately fell a victim to her motherly charm. By the time she died she was indeed the "Mater Patriae", and she has come to represent the epitome of all that is specifically "Austrian" in Austrian life and institutions.

Her son Joseph II (1780—1790), who had been co-Regent since his father's death in 1765, was now in sole command and at once decided to speed up the reforms his mother had initiated, and did not shrink from applying them to Hungary as well. He was undoubtedly a man of vision and integrity, and much more approachable than any previous Habsburg had been. After he had thrown open the Vienna Prater to the public in 1766, he was asked why he spent so much time associating with the "lower orders": he is said to have replied that if he were

Hos, O Diva, tibi Natura in corpore vultus
    pectore plus, totum se dedit ipse DEVS.
Quid mirum pro te mundus quod certet, et æther
    parte colunt ambo te meliore DEAM.

The Empress Maria Theresia, by Martin v. Meytens

Andreas Hofer

to mix only with his equals he would have to spend the rest of his life in the Habsburg vault of the Capuchin church in Vienna. What he aimed at, by and large, was a Welfare State governed by Reason and administered by enlightened bureaucrats headed by himself. The spate of reforms was positively torrential. Apart from the abolition of serfdom and torture most of them were concerned with religion. The crime of heresy was done away with, and henceforth religion was to be regarded as a matter for the individual to decide for himself without State interference. The Church was to be subservient to the State, and religious toleration was to include the emancipation of the Jews (this in face of the implacable anti-Semitism of the Court) and the legality of civil marriage. There was hardly a detail of ecclesiastical life that was not affected in one way or another, even down to precise regulations about the number of candles per church, or about the amount of ritual and ostentation permissible at funerals. Even the location and measurements of graves were subjected to official control. As for the vast central Civil Service that he envisaged (with himself at its head), all its work was to be conducted in German: German was to be the one official language in even the remotest part of his scattered domains.

In all this, of course, he was far ahead of his times, indeed he anticipated the "Welfare State" by about 150 years. But just as the opera "Der Rosenkavalier" epitomises the age of Maria Theresia, so the moral drawn by one of its principal characters exactly fits Joseph II: "It's the 'how' that makes the difference." All these worthy and in many cases overdue reforms were introduced with an excess of zeal and a want of tact that antagonized practically every section of the community. He antagonized his advisers by his insistence that Reason must prevail. He antagonized the nobility by creating an atmosphere of commotion and instability in which constructive planning was impossible, nor did he succeed in placating them by handing out titles to bankers and industrialists. He antagonized his mother by largely undoing all the solid, patient work she had put in, and their almost perpetual disagreements soon became a by-word. Worst of all he even succeeded in antagonizing the Pope, Pius VI, who in 1782 took the unprecedented step of travelling to Vienna in person to ensure that Joseph's drastic Church reforms were curtailed, the last straw being the Emperor's closure of over 700 monasteries and the confiscation of their property.

Joseph has gone down to history as the "Enlightened Despot" but this is perhaps not quite fair: a kinder assessment would be "The people's Emperor". He honestly wanted to improve the lot of the "plebs misera", the masses, but like other reformers he went the wrong way about it. He wanted to run before he had learned to walk, to turn the whole State into a vast machine without any understanding of human nature. In riding roughshod over tradition and custom he showed none of his mother's political flair and little of her humanity. His reforms were imposed with such recklessness and impetuosity that they defeated their own object; and if it would be going too far to say that the effect of his rashness was actually to encourage reaction and retard his mother's progressive reforms, there is no question that he left Austria disunited and in a social and political ferment. Shortly before the end of his life frustation seems to have yielded to resignation: at all events he composed his own highly appropriate epitaph: "Here lies a Prince whose intentions were honest but who had the misfortune to see all his projects miscarry." In other words, he meant well, but . . .

CHAPTER FIVE

Napoleon, the Congress of Vienna and Metternich

Austria	Elsewhere
	1789 Surrender of the Bastille in Paris.
1790–92 Leopold II.	
1791 *Death of Mozart and birth of Grillparzer.*	1791–92 *Joseph Haydn in London.*
1792–1835 The Emperor Franz.	1793 Execution of Marie Antoinette.
1794 *Beethoven settles in Vienna.*	
	1794 Execution of Robespierre and Danton.
1795 Third Partition of Poland: Austria acquires West Galicia and Cracow, and Poland is obliterated.	1794–95 *Joseph Haydn in London.*
1795 *The Albertina founded.*	
1797 Treaty of Campo Formio: Austria loses Belgium and receives Venetia, Istria and Dalmatia.	
1797–1828 *Franz Schubert.*	1798 Battle of the Nile.
1799 *Haydn's Oratorio "The Creation".*	1799 Death of George Washington.
1803 Secularisation of Salzburg.	
	1804 Napoleon makes himself Emperor.
1805 Battle of Austerlitz and Treaty of Pressburg: Austria loses Tyrol and Venetia. First French occupation of Vienna.	1805 Battle of Trafalgar.
1806 The Emperor Franz renounces the crown of the Holy Roman Empire, which comes to an end.	
	1807 The French occupy Portugal.
	1808 Napoleon's brother Joseph King of Spain.
1809 Tyrol's fight for freedom (Andreas Hofer).	1809 Birth of Abraham Lincoln.

Austria	*Elsewhere*
1809 Second French occupation of Vienna. Battles of Aspern and Wagram. Treaty of Vienna. *Death of Joseph Haydn.*	
1810 Marriage of the Emperor Franz's daughter Marie Louise to Napoleon.	
1810–48 Metternich Chancellor.	1812 Napoleon's retreat from Moscow.
1813 Battle of Leipzig.	1813 *Birth of Wagner and Verdi.*
1814 *First performance of the revised version of Beethoven's opera "Fidelio".*	1814 Napoleon banished to Elba.
1814–15 Congress of Vienna: Salzburg, Tyrol and Vorarlberg restored to Austria.	
1815 The "Holy Alliance" between Austria, Russia and Prussia. *The Vienna Polytechnic is founded.*	1815 The Battle of Waterloo.
1815–48 *The "Biedermeier" era.*	
	1818 Birth of Karl Marx.
	1821 Death of Napoleon at St. Helena.
	1823 The Monroe Doctrine.
1824 *Completion of the Arlberg Pass.* *Birth of Anton Bruckner at Ansfelden, Upper Austria.*	
1825 *Birth of Johann Strauss (the younger).*	
1827 *Death of Beethoven.*	
1828 *Death of Schubert.*	
1829 First trials of a screw-driven vessel in Trieste harbour.	
1830 Birth at Schönbrunn of the future Emperor Franz Joseph I.	
	1832 *Death of Goethe.*
	1834 Death of Lafayette.
1835–48 Ferdinand I ("The Amiable").	
	1837 Accession of Queen Victoria of England.
	1838 Death of Talleyrand.

Austria	Elsewhere
1839 *Austria's first railway.* *Madersperger invents the* *sewing-machine.* 1842 *First "Philharmonic" con-* *cert in Vienna.*	
	1846–78 Pope Pius IX.
1848 March: uprising in Vienna. May: Court retires to Inns- bruck, but returns in Au- gust. Metternich flees to Lon- don. Field-Marshal Radetzky (1766–1858) retrieves the situation in the Italian Provinces. October: a second up- rising in Vienna. The Court moves to Olomouc in Moravia where the Em- peror Ferdinand abdicates and is succeeded by Franz Joseph I.	1848 The Risorgimento in Italy. Revolt in Hungary under Lajos Kossuth.

When writing of Napoleon it is impossible, as the great English man of letters Dr. Samuel Johnson observed in a rather different context, "to say anything new that is true, or anything true that is new". It is not however impossible to emphasise certain features of the Napoleonic era that are not generally realised, and one of them is that with the exception of England Austria was in the field against Napoleon longer than any other country in Europe. She was also the first to feel the full fury of revolutionary France's military power, and the war that France declared in 1792 lasted with only a few "breathers" right up till 1813.

At the outset Austria was not without allies and faced the French with the support of Prussia, Holland and Spain, but the Prussians, not liking the look of things at all, made a separate peace in 1795 and left the Austrians to bear the brunt of the land fighting. Their armies proved no match for the genius of the young Napoleon, who chased them out of the whole of Italy and right up into northern Styria. By the Peace of Campo Formio in 1797 Austria ceded Belgium to France and lost Lombardy, but was compensated with Venetia, Istria and Dalmatia, the 1000 year old Republic of Venice being obliterated.

After desultory fighting had flared up at intervals between 1799 and 1802, Austria felt strong enough by 1805 to take the field again, this time in the company of England, Russia and Sweden against France, Bavaria and Württemberg. The results were even more catastrophic: an entire Austrian army capitulated at Ulm, Napoleon occupied Vienna, and then annihilated the Austrians and Russians at the Battle of Austerlitz in Moravia in 1805, one of his most tremendous victories. This time the terms of the Peace Treaty (at Pressburg) were less lenient: Austria had to cede all her Italian possessions, and lost Tyrol and Vorarlberg to Bavaria. In return she received Salzburg, which had been secularised in 1803, the last Prince-Archbishop, the same Hieronymus von Colleredo who had given Mozart such short shift in 1781, being awarded the Grand-Duchy of Würzburg. As if this were not enough, the Emperor Franz was forced to lay aside the crown of the Holy Roman Empire, which Habsburgs had worn continuously since 1438 with the exception of the three years 1742—1745. From now on the Emperors took the title of Emperor of Austria.

Following the Treaty of Pressburg in 1805, the Emperor's brother, the Archduke Karl, undertook a thorough reorganisation of the Austrian army, but it was from a very different quarter that the next revolt against Napoleon was organised.

Tyrol had been part of Austria since 1363, and the "Land in the Mountains" lying astride important north-

70

south and east-west lines of communications was one of the brightest jewels in the Habsburg crown, specially distinguished for its unswerving loyalty to the ruling House of Austria. Of all the stipulations of the Treaty of Pressburg after the disastrous "Battle of the Three Emperors" at Austerlitz the most painful was the clause detaching Tyrol from Austria and grafting it on to the Kingdom of Bavaria which had been created out of the domains of the defunct Holy Roman Empire. Even the temporary acquisition of Salzburg was poor consolation for the loss of Tyrol. The blunders of the Bavarian administration soon provoked widespread discontent in Tyrol, every detail of which was carefully recorded in Vienna. Imperial agents were smuggled into the Province from Salzburg and Klagenfurt; the bonds of loyalty which still linked the "Land in the Mountains" with the Austrian Emperor were assiduously strengthened, and the discontent was kept smouldering and seething with an eye to the eventual renewal of hostilities against Napoleon. From 1805 on, the rising temperature of the Tyrolese people became a prime factor in the plan of campaign being drawn up by the Imperial War Council in Vienna, plans in which the Tyrolese militia were to have a definite part to play. The driving force behind the mobilisation of Tyrol's determination to be free was the Archduke Johann, another brother of the Emperor Franz. By March 1806 the Emperor had been acquainted with the plans for a national uprising in Tyrol, and towards the end of 1808, when the decision to renew hostilities against Napoleon had already been taken, the Archduke Johann informed the Emperor of his plans, in which Tyrol was not specifically mentioned, but "the principal object in view was undoubtedly Tyrol". The time had now come to work out a definite plan of action: spies and agents were no longer enough, what was now required was personal contact. And so three men were chosen to go to Vienna as representatives of the people of

Tyrol: Andreas Hofer from the Passeier valley and Huber from Bruneck, both innkeepers, and Nessing, a coffee-house owner from Bozen, all from South Tyrol. All three were widely known in Tyrol, and their work (Hofer was a cattle-dealer, Huber was a herbalist, and Nessing was the secretary of the Bozen Traders' Association) enabled them to circulate freely throughout Tyrol without exciting suspicion; so that eventually they succeeded in slipping out of Tyrol undetected by the Bavarian authorities and in making their way to Vienna, which they reached towards the end of January 1809. It was of course essential that their presence in the capital should be kept as secret as possible, which in view of Hofer's striking appearance, with his great black beard and his Tyrolese national costume, was no easy matter. During their six days's stay in Vienne, the delegates had three long conferences with the Archduke Johann, and by the time they left the capital on 2 February the parts they were to play in the forthcoming fight for freedom were clearly determined. In fulfilling his mission in Vienna Andreas Hofer had shown considerable aptitude and reliability; back in Tyrol, preparations for the uprising were pushed ahead cautiously but effectively, and detailed instructions circulated from village to village.

Although the Bavarian authorities had got wind of the visit to Vienna, they were completely in the dark as to its purpose. The cumbersome communications systems of those days, and the rigidity of the Bavarian government in Tyrol, effectively precluded any premature leakage of the plans for the revolt. The Tyrolese militia was to be at readiness by 12 March; but it was April before the Imperial Austrian troops were ready. The rising in Tyrol took place precisely according to plan: in a series of heroic battles the Bavarian army of occupation and the French troops hurrying to their assistance were everywhere thrown back and finally forced to surrender on 12 April 1809 at the first battle of Berg Isel, just outside the Tyrolese capital of Innsbruck. And so for the first time in this "annus mirabilis" 1809 Tyrol had liberated herself by her own exertions, without the Imperial Austrian forces making any appreciable contribution to the victory.

But scarcely had the last echo of the celebrations and thanksgivings throughout Tyrol died away than the Imperial Austrian troops were in full retreat and Tyrol had to be abandoned to the enemy's vengeance while Napoleon advanced on Vienna with his main force.

On 13 May Napoleon entered Vienna and installed himself in the Imperial summer residence at Schönbrunn. On 21 May he suffered his first defeat at the bloody battle of Aspern, against Archduke Karl's Austrian army. Meanwhile in Tyrol beacon-fires on the mountain-tops and alarm bells from the church-tops were once more calling the people to arms in defence of their liberty, but after an engagement near Wörgl in which they suffered severe losses a small force of Imperial Austrian troops withdrew, so that once again the full brunt of the struggle had to be borne by the Tyrolese peasants, armed as often as not with scythes and billhooks and other agricultural implements. One worthy is even said to have brandished a heavy wooden crucifix studded with nails.

It was at this juncture that Andreas Hofer's stature grew from that of a local leader of the volunteer contingent from the Passeier valley to that of a unanimously acclaimed leader of the whole people. After the pitiable failure of the Imperial Austrian troops and their leaders, Hofer was approached by well-known personages from all parts of the Province imploring him in this hour of need to take the defence of Tyrol into his own hands. Andreas Hofer had never aspired to leadership; it was thrust upon him by the people, who placed the fullest confidence in him.

His outward appearance was certainly impressive; he

was tall and massive in frame, with a great black beard which gave him an appearance of dignity far beyond his years, and he always wore the traditional costume of his native valley. In this year of destiny 1809 he was in his 42nd year, having been born in 1767. What won the complete confidence of the peasants was simply and solely Hofer's character: they obeyed him, they followed his instructions, and it was due entirely to his moderation and leniency that the uprising never degenerated into an exchange of atrocities. Clumsy in bureaucratic affairs, when it came to choosing a position or formulating a plan for throwing the invader back across the frontiers Hofer showed his inborn instinct for turning the mountains to the best possible advantage by the use of previously prepared avalanches. His outlook never ranged very much further than the mountains of his native land, and despite his fanatical loyalty to the Emperor he had only the haziest idea of what was meant by "Austria"; but his stature grew to match the magnitude of the task allotted to him, and when all Tyrol looked to him, and to him alone, he stood firm as a rock amid the surrounding turmoil.

And so once again on 29 May 1809 the Tyrolese levies, obedient to the call, routed the punitive Franco-Bavarian expedition in the bloody second battle of Berg Isel and compelled them to evacuate Tyrol. Once again, as in the glorious days of April, the land was free, and with the publication in mid-June of a letter addressed from the Emperor at Wolkersdorf to the people of Tyrol, containing the solemn promise "never to sign any Peace Treaty which does not guarantee the indissoluble union of your land with my domains" Tyrol was borne on a flood-tide of exultant confidence. Small wonder that, intoxicated by the heady delights of liberation, the people of Tyrol paid little heed to growing reports of armistice negotiations in Vienna, treating all such rumours as malicious enemy propaganda.

But in actual fact the supreme commander of the Imperial forces, Archduke Karl, was compelled by Napoleon's hard-won victory at Wagram, following Karl's victory at Aspern, to conclude an armistice on 12 July by the terms of which Tyrol was specifically to be handed over to the avenging sword of the victors. This armistice, dictated by military expediency, was bitterly criticised by the Emperor, especially the abandonment of Tyrol: "What causes me particular grief is the violation of my honour, in that I abandoned to their fate the valiant people of Tyrol, who have given their all in the cause, in almost the self-same moment as I assured them of my staunchest support": and the Emperor's anger led to the Archduke Karl's resignation as commander-in-chief. The armistice did indeed deliver Tyrol into the hands of the avenger; in fact, the desire for vengeance was Napoleon's principal motive in ceasing hostilities. "My main reason for concluding an armistice," he wrote to Marshal Lefebvre (whom he had detached from his main force with precise instructions about the treatment to be meted out to Tyrol), "was the subjugation of Tyrol. I hope you will soon be able to report to me that you have beaten down, dispersed and disarmed the people of this land."

In mid-July the French general Lefebvre advanced into Tyrol at the head of 50,000 men, and such slight resistance as he encountered was broken with brutal ferocity: Schwaz and many other places were burnt to the ground, and on 30 July he entered Innsbruck, the remnants of the Austrian troops and the Imperial administration having already left the Province. From his headquarters at Innsbruck Lefebvre began to plan the systematic subjugation of the land, but was soon forced to realise that the capture of Innsbruck was one thing, but the conquest of the whole Province was quite a different matter. The columns which he despatched into the mountain valleys encountered ferocious resistance at all points; stoutly defended defiles, broken bridges, roads made impassable, and up in the mountains an invisible but seemingly ubiquitous enemy whose strength grew from day to day. At the third and bloodiest battle of Berg Isel on 13 August, the mountains surrounding Innsbruck remained firmly in Tyrolese hands, a resounding victory indeed. More than any other single event during this year of battles the August battle of Berg Isel attracted the attention of the outside world, and especially of Germany and England, where the news of Tyrol's revolt, which had been followed with growing interest, was received with admiration and enthusiasm.

"Oberkommandant" Andreas Hofer now took up residence in the Hofburg at Innsbruck, where he set himself to master administrative problems with which he was totally unfamiliar, and to restore some sort of order to the government of the Province, which had been completely disorganised by successive upheavals. As to Vienna making peace overtures, Andreas Hofer implicitly believed the Emperor's word, never to conclude any peace involving the separation of Tyrol from Austria: his trust in his Emperor was as dogged and whole-hearted as his trust in the beliefs of his forefathers. It was only natural that he should turn a deaf ear to the rumours which began to circulate through Tyrol — that peace negotiations were afoot and that Tyrol was once more to be torn from Austria. All such rumours were surely malicious distortions, deliberately put about by the French and Bavarians to confuse the Tyrolese?

But in point of fact peace was signed at Schönbrunn on 14 October 1809; once again Tyrol was torn from Austria, and divided up into three parts. The Tyrolese were promised an amnesty if they laid down their arms, but how could they bring themselves to believe that things had really come to such a pass? Now was the moment when a definite statement from the Emperor was required. A draft proclamation ordering the people of Tyrol to lay

76

down their arms had already been submitted to the Emperor Franz, but he never signed it. A clear lead from the Emperor at the proper time would at once have dissipated all the confused rumours and false reports that were flying about Tyrol; that he failed to give such a lead is to the Emperor's discredit. In time, news of the peace treaty naturally filtered through, and the calmer and more prudent elements among the population abandoned the struggle forthwith; but the hotheads and firebrands joined together in a new revolt. The last volunteer force which Tyrol, ravaged and bleeding to death, was able to raise was of sturdy enough quality; what was lacking was the former sense of complete unity. And so against his better judgment and with no sure confidence in victory Andreas Hofer agreed to resume the fight.

Strong enemy columns were pushing forward into Tyrol from three directions at once. Hofer's plan was the same as before, to concentrate the entire Tyrolese forces at Berg Isel and there await the enemy; but this time he was overruled in the peasants' council of war. Aimlessness, uncertainty and disunity hamstrung any effective decision, and the small volunteer bands defending their native valleys were easily routed by the superior forces of the advancing enemy. Making one last appeal to the population, Hofer also turned once more to the Emperor: "The idea that Your Majesty can have been unmindful of us when making peace is unthinkable: Tyrol is ready, I warrant, to shed the last drop of her blood for Your Majesty." But the Emperor was far from Tyrol, far away in central Hungary. And so the tragedy had to be played out. On 1 November, for the fourth time in this memorable year, the defenders of Tyrol assembled at Berg Isel to await the enemy. But "Oberkommandant" Hofer was at Matrei, four hours' journey from the field of battle, in a mood of abject resignation, tortured by doubts and anxieties, without any plan or purpose. The engagement at Berg Isel was brief;

the Tyrolese were defeated, and with symptoms of despondency and disintegration becoming only too apparent, Hofer was prepared to sign a capitulation. A few days later however he was talked round by a group of hotheads into withdrawing his signature, and once more issued a call to arms. This duplicity put a price upon his head: his followers were scattered, and he himself sought refuge in a South Tyrol mountain lair, the Pfandleralm near Brantach in St. Martin in the Passeier valley. Why he made no attempt to flee the country or to give himself up to the French general remains a mystery; the latter had given him his word that not a hair of his head should be touched if he gave himself up. Instead, he remained in his hide-out even after he knew that it had been betrayed to the enemy. On 27 January 1810 French soldiers were conducted to the hide-out by a traitor and Hofer gave himself up without a struggle. He was taken to Mantua and on instructions from Napoleon shot on 20 February 1810.

Hofer's behaviour during the last weeks of the uprising can only be explained by a tragic mental confusion from which he could find no way out. With the final general collapse of 1809 Hofer must have lost all confidence in himself. How could a simple, right-thinking, unassuming peasant comprehend that his Emperor, in whose name he had issued so many orders, endured so many hardships and undertaken so much responsibility, for whose throne he had led so many of his compatriots to death on the battlefield, his Emperor who had solemnly promised never to consent to the separation of Tyrol and who only a few weeks previously had rewarded him with a medal of honour, could be capable of breaking his word? This was the tragedy in which Hofer was caught up, and which eventually led him in desperation to the final, senseless act of resistance.

In point of fact, by the autumn of 1809 the Emperor was no longer in a position to give Tyrol any help. The war was lost, Napoleon was installed in Schönbrunn, the Austrian domains were in enemy hands. The realities of the situation soon became known in Tyrol, and should have counselled prudence and a readiness to face facts and accept the inevitable; but is it fair to expect a people who had risen four times in one year in furious revolt against a numerically superior enemy in defence of their country's liberty and of their loyalty to their Emperor: is it fair to expect such a people to be capable of taking a calm, objective view of the situation? The blame rests squarely on the Emperor for his failure to give a lead during the last hour of Tyrol's struggle.

One of Napoleon's first actions on entering Vienna had been to give instructions that every consideration was to be accorded to the aged Joseph Haydn, including a military guard outside his house in the western suburbs where he died in his sleep on 31 May 1809. And before leaving Schönbrunn Napoleon saw to it that his tenure was commemorated by two eagles on each side of the main entrance, and no Austrian Government has ever bothered to have these symbols of foreign domination removed from their lofty perch above the great courtyard: if they are decorative, why take them down?

Comfortably installed in Schönbrunn Palace in Vienna Napoleon dictated the terms of yet another Peace Treaty with Austria — and this time he was determined to stand no more nonsense from these Austrians. Salzburg and part of Upper Austria went to Bavaria, and a new Kingdom of Illyria was constituted, consisting of Carniola, Istria (with Fiume and Trieste) and parts of Carinthia. Tyrol, its people having been duly "beaten down, dispersed and disarmed", was divided (as Caesar divided Gaul) into three parts: North Tyrol to Bavaria, South Tyrol to Italy, and East Tyrol to Illyria. Compared with these humiliating dismemberments, which left Austria without any access to the sea, the cession of Western Galicia to the Grand Duchy of Warsaw seemed merely incidental.

It was against this sombre background, when Austria's fortunes were at their lowest ebb, that the great Klemens Lothar Metternich appears upon the scene. Previously he had been Austrian Ambassador in Paris, where he had been on terms of friendship with a French diplomat of equal stature, Prince Talleyrand. He was therefore no stranger to French aspirations and immediately set about blunting them with a policy of appeasement. Appointed Imperial Chancellor in 1810 he succeeded in persuading the unpretentious Emperor Franz to agree to a marriage in Vienna between his daughter Marie Louise and Napoleon himself, who had just disposed of Josephine. The eventual issue of this union was the unhappy Duke of Reichstadt (1811—1832), who remained virtually a prisoner in Schönbrunn for the whole of his short life. Next, Metternich carried his apparent appeasement to the lengths of agreeing to contribute a small Austrian contingent to Napoleon's disastrous Moscow expedition of 1812, perhaps foreseeing that Napoleon might be more amenable to negotiation after it than in his post-Austerlitz mood.

And so it proved; Metternich talked Napoleon into granting an armistice which gave Austria a breathing space to reform her armies, and then offered to mediate with peace proposals to both sides, France on the one hand, and Prussia and Russia on the other. At the same time he let it be known that Austria would intervene against whichever side declined to accept his proposals. Prussia and Russia agreed, Napoleon in a stormy scene at Dresden did not; whereupon Metternich declared war on France at the side of Prussia and Russia, the allied forces being under the supreme command of the Austrian Prince Karl Schwarzenberg, with Josef Radetzky (1766—1858), who was to be responsible for quelling the uprising in Italy some 35 years later, as Chief of Staff. At the Battle of Leipzig in 1813 Napoleon suffered the bloodiest defeat of his life: on 31 March 1814 Friedrich Wilhelm of Prussia and the Czar Alexander of Russia rode into Paris, and on 11 April Napoleon abdicated and was packed off to the island of Elba. To Metternich must go the credit for the brilliant diplomacy that led up to Napoleon's defeat, and for the leniency and far-sightedness of the Treaty of Paris, which included no territorial concessions or reparations of any kind. What it did include was a Clause calling for a European Congress in Vienna, within two months, to work out a final settlement of Europe.

By the end of the year the crowned heads of Europe and the enormous retinues they were accustomed to travel about with were comfortably ensconced in Vienna, and the Congress had appointed a Committee of the Big Four (Russia, England, Prussia and Austria) and unanimously elected Metternich as its President. Metternich's first action was to have the French representative Talleyrand co-opted on to the Committee on equal terms with the others.

And that is about as far as the Congress got — in public at any rate. But the famous *bon mot* coined by Charles Joseph Lamoral, Prince de Ligne, about the Congress dancing but not making any progress was in fact rather wide of the mark. It was precisely because there was so much dancing that so much progress *was* made — behind the scenes. Diplomacy is usually most successful when it is in secret, and many a ticklish problem was resolved in private conversations during a stroll in the Prater or over the glacis, or even in some elegant boudoir or other. This Prince de Ligne, the doyen of the Congress, had a sense of humour which even on his death bed was as irrepressible as ever: he claimed that the Congress should be grateful to him for being about to provide it with the only chance it was ever likely to have of seeing an Austrian Field-Marshal's funeral.

One of the many lampoons that went the rounds during the Congress purported to show how the work of the Congress was apportioned:

> the Czar of Russia to do all the love-making,
> the King of Prussia to do all the thinking,
> the King of Denmark to do all the talking,
> the King of Bavaria to do all the drinking,
> the King of Württemberg to do all the eating,
> and the Emperor Franz of Austria to pay for it all.

Indeed, the Congress was costing the thrifty Franz something like 50,000 gulden a day, and to make matters worse he and his family had to move out of the Hofburg to provide accommodation for his guests, as well as putting up his daughter Marie-Louise, now a grass-widow, and her small son the Duke of Reichstadt. What with one thing and another poor Franz had more than his fair share of indignities to put up with: the execution of his aunt, Marie-Antoinette, and her husband King Louis XVI of France, followed by the forced marriage of his daughter Marie-Louise to Napoleon; Napoleon's occupation of Schönbrunn; and finally being forced to lay aside the Crown of the Holy Roman Empire. And now, as the Congress' host, he had to cut a public figure instead of leading the simple, unpretentious life which he longed for after the turmoil and humiliations of the long war. It went against the grain to have to spend such vast sums on pomp and pageantry. But none of the guests could complain of any shortage of entertainment. The indefatigable Czar was said to have been out dancing 40 nights running, with the King of Denmark a close second. During the day-time there were tournaments and parades in the Prater, or elaborate shooting parties in the Vienna Woods at which protocol was strictly observed: first Emperors would loose off, then the Kings would have a go, and any animal lucky enough to survive both these broadsides would suffer the indignity of being polished off by a mere Prince.

In the evenings the aristocracy — families such as Esterházy, Palffy, Auersperg, Schwarzenberg, Lobkowitz, Kinsky, Liechtenstein, etc. — kept open house, while at the Rasumofsky residence there was as likely as not chamber music by Ludwig van Beethoven. It was on 25 January 1815 that Beethoven himself conducted a gala concert of his own works in the Rittersaal of the Hofburg, the same hall in which his Eighth Symphony had been performed for the first time on almost exactly the same date the year before. With his aristocratic connections Beethoven was one of the social lions of the Congress — if he was in the mood. And Franz Schubert? Apart from a small circle of friends Schubert was not even a name, though those in the know claimed to have heard somewhere or other that he had turned out one or two promising songs.

All this social and boudoir activity meant that at its plenary sessions, attended by representatives of over 200 countries, dynasties, principalities and communities (including the exotic Prince of Lebanon) there was little to be done except to ratify settlements already agreed upon in private conversation or dalliance. There were only two questions over which the Congress really got bogged down: Saxony and Poland. Metternich's policy of balance of power in Europe, with the full support of the English delegate Lord Castlereagh, could not agree to the whole of Saxony being awarded to Prussia for fear of a repetition of Frederick "the Great's" violation of Silesia. And to allow Russia to lay hands on the Grand Duchy of Warsaw was to risk the eventual erosion of Austrian Galicia and Cracow. In the end, compromises were arrived at: as Bismarck observed many years later, "Metternich cut up countries like old pairs of trousers".

As far as Austria was concerned, her long service in the field against Napoleon was rewarded by Lombardy

(Milan), Venice, Dalmatia, Illyria and Galicia, in return for the cession of Belgium and scattered territories in south-west Germany. She also recovered Salzburg, Tyrol and Vorarlberg. These transactions brought Austria an increase in population of some $4\frac{1}{2}$ million, and the undisputed hegemony in Italy. Furthermore, Austria was elected President of the loose "German Confederation". Politically, they meant a pronounced shift eastwards of Austria's centre of gravity, to the Danube and northern Italy.

With all these agreements signed, sealed and settled, the Congress was about to be informed of a secret alliance between Austria, England and France, when a dramatic message was whispered into Metternich's ear that reduced the assembly to the stature of a historical curiosity: Napoleon had escaped from Elba and was marching on Paris. After the first stunned silence the Congress for once got busy; outstanding business was summarily wound up, the Grand Alliance was reconstituted on the spot, Talleyrand on behalf of Louis XVIII placed himself at the Allies' disposal, and the captains and the Kings departed, leaving the Emperor Franz to foot the bill.

After the Congress of Vienna Austria enjoyed a prestige in Europe she never again attained. It was the last time Austria was to play a dominant role in European affairs, thanks to the flair and tenacity of Klemens Lothar Metternich, the most brilliant diplomat of his time. When he first became Chancellor in 1810 Austria was all but down and out; within ten years he had made Vienna the political capital of Europe, and by the time he fell from power in 1848 Austria and Europe could look back on over 30 years of unbroken peace.

After the fall of Napoleon, he took over the apparatus Kaunitz had built up and proceeded to organise his famous "system" against any influence that could possibly subvert the stability of the Austrian Empire. His arch-enemy was nationalism, to which a multi-racial State like Austria was particularly vulnerable. He was quite prepared to join the Czar Alexander's mystical "Holy Alliance" of Austria, Russia and Prussia provided he could at the same time continue close co-operation with England, who would have nothing to do with it, and with France. The keystones of his policy were peace, stability, and the preservation of the status quo, and after all the upheavals of the preceding twenty years such a policy was bound to be popular, for the time being at any rate. He was convinced that Austria, at the heart of Europe, must be strong enough to preserve the balance of power he had so assiduously built up. And for nearly thirty years Austria was the leading political force in Europe, and Metternich the uncrowned King of the German-speaking world. But it was not enough to keep Austria strong, there had to be stability in the neighbouring countries too; and nationalism had to be rigorously suppressed for fear of contagion. The slightest symptom of revolution was to be instantly nipped in the bud. An eye had to be kept on Germany and Italy, though Metternich refused to regard Italy as more than "a geographical expression". Slav aspirations had to be curbed, and above all the tiresome Hungarians had to be brought to heel. In all this he was successful, and under his "system" Austria enjoyed an era of peace and material prosperity in which there was an abundance of all the good things of life — except freedom. There was no free Parliament, no free Press, no free University, no intelligent Civil Service. Any ideas remotely savouring of liberalism were suppressed. For all his brilliance as a diplomat, where Metternich failed as a statesman was in his failure, or refusal, to understand that revolution was not the only alternative to autocracy. In his view, and in the Emperor's too, anything liberal or progressive was dangerous, and it was his horror of revolution that automatically involved him in the suppression of liberty. The fact that the Emperor, the "gute alte Franz", was anything but a forceful personality, suited his purpose admirably. And when Franz died in 1835 Metternich saw to it that his son Ferdinand duly succeeded to the throne despite the fact that he was far too simple-minded to be able to cope with the affairs of State, for it meant that a Regency Council could be set up consisting of the Archduke Ludwig (Ferdinand's uncle); the Archduke Franz Karl (Ferdinand's brother); Graf Kolowrat, an opponent of Metternich's, to be in charge of financial affairs; and Metternich himself. So Ferdinand "the amiable" was an invaluable figure-head, and goes down to history as a charming, excessively gullible and well-meaning individual who was adored by his subjects and made no difficulties when in 1848 it was put to him that he might be happier living in retirement as a private citizen instead of being confused by all these tiresome revolutions.

So Metternich continued to rule through the Crown, the Church, the Army, and above all the secret police and the censorship. In his own words, he was "shoring up a building on the verge of dilapidation", "plugging cracks" and "stopping dry-rot". Or as the Emperor Franz put it: "My realm is like a worm-eaten house: if any part of it is moved there is no knowing how much will collapse." By the 1840's Metternich must have realised that he was prescribing soporifics and bromides instead of the surgical treatment that was urgently necessary. But after putting the clock back Metternich then stopped it altogether. His "system" congealed into a rigid, unyielding autocracy. He thought he could ride the storm of the nationalist liberal movements, and was firmly convinced he could take the wind out of their sails with a few minor reforms. True, he was well aware where the weakness of the Monarchy lay, and he held in his own hands the remedies for the ills it was beset by, only he no longer had the strength to apply them. That was his tragedy. The sequel was inevitable. Metternich carried on with the dignity of a "grand seigneur" until the collapse of his "system" buried him under its own ruins. In 1848, when the simmering revolution at last boiled over, Metternich made his escape to London, and did not return until 1851, when the situation was firmly under control. He lived on until 1859, and although living in retirement was still a power behind the scenes until his death at the age of 86.

Metternich was gifted with a brilliant personality, a cool head, quick and far-seeing perception, firmness and patriotism. He gave his name to a whole era, and with all his faults he did succeed in keeping his country at peace for over 30 years. And after his fall came the age of imperialism that led to two World Wars. Perhaps the best verdict is the Austrian writer Franz Grillparzer's: "A very great diplomat but not a great statesman."

The cultural counterpart of the "Metternich era" was "Biedermeier", a phenomenon virtually confined to the Austria of 1815—1848. Originally applied only to painting, and more particularly to furniture, the word later came to be associated with a whole way of life. It was a direct result of the failure to proceed with the reforms Maria Theresia had started, and of the increasing material prosperity of the middle-classes. In Metternich's police-State the middle-classes were not allowed to take a hand in the conduct of affairs; politics was a matter for professionals only: so the middle-classes had plenty of time on their hands to devote to the home and the family. Biedermeier represents a reaction from the exuberance of baroque and the flamboyance of rococo towards homely simplicity and unpretentiousness. Comfort and above all respectability were the order of the day, with cosy parlours and plenty of good food and wine, if possible in the open-air. Another feature of Biedermeier life was "Hausmusik", music-making at home, the kind of gathering immortalised in the famous "Schubertiades". Music and theatre (heavily censored of course, as Grillparzer found to his cost) were encouraged by the authorities to keep people's minds off politics, to divert them from "dangerous thoughts". And with the waltzes of Johann Strauss and Josef Lanner to dance to, the middle-classes certainly showed little inclination to bother their heads about politics, which is just what "the Establishment" wanted. So there was work and security and a good time for all, and everyone was happy — except perhaps the intelligentsia.

And it was the intelligentsia who eventually struck. In Vienna, the overture to the turbulent year 1848 was a demonstration of students and professors from the University who made their way, not to the Hofburg, for they had nothing against the amiable Emperor, but to near Metternich's residence, to present demands for a free Press and trial by jury.

Metternich resigned and made his way to London after having to hide in a laundry-cart. Far more serious were the risings in other parts of the Empire, and as usual it was the Hungarians who made the running, inspired by their fiery leader Lajos Kossuth. As soon as the news of the disturbances in Vienna reached Milan, all the Italian Provinces rose as one man and Field-Marshal Radetzky's army was forced to abandon Milan. Next the Czechs set up a Government of their own in Prague, and by May the situation was so threatening that Ferdinand and his Court were evacuated to Innsbruck, where they stayed until August while Prince Albert Windischgrätz used artillery to restore order in Prague. In July the veteran Field-Marshal Radetzky retrieved the situation in Italy by routing the Piedmontese at the Battle of Custozza.

All these disturbances were due primarily to pan-Slav nationalism among the Czechs and Croats, and to the explosive patriotism of the Hungarians and Italians. The riots in Vienna on the other hand were partly an inevitable reaction to the long years during which freedom had been stifled, and partly the result of economic hardship among the peasants brought about by the last years of Metternich's "system". Though directed first and foremost against Metternich, the risings nearly toppled the uncomprehending Emperor Ferdinand, and it needed the cool head and iron determination of the Archduchess Sophie of Bavaria, the mother of the future Emperor Franz Joseph, to hold the Court together. In view of the alarming situation in Hungary, which had proclaimed its secession, it was deemed advisable for the Court to be evacuated again, this time to the sizeable town of Olomouc in Moravia, while Windischgrätz restored order in Vienna after a bombardment in which parts of the Hofburg were set on fire. Meanwhile an army under the command of Joseph Jellačić, the Governor of Croatia, consisting mainly of Croats who were longing to get some of their own back on their Hungarian oppressors, took the offensive against Kossuth's Hungarian forces, but it was not until well on into 1849 that the Hungarians were eventually subdued by Prince Felix Schwarzenberg, the brother-in-law of Windischgrätz, with the help of no fewer than 200,000 Russian troops hastily called in under the terms of the "Holy Alliance" of 1815. And by that time Ferdinand at Olomouc had made no difficulties about abdicating and had given his blessing to Austria's new Emperor Franz Joseph I, aged 18.

CHAPTER SIX

Franz Joseph I, 1848–1916

Austria	Elsewhere
1854 Marriage of Franz Joseph I and Elisabeth of Bavaria in Vienna. *Opening of the Semmering railway.*	1853–56 Crimean War.
1856 *Birth of Sigmund Freud.*	1856 *Birth of Oscar Wilde and Bernhard Shaw*
1856–90 *The modernisation of Vienna: construction of the Ringstrasse and the buildings along it.*	
1858 Birth of Crown Prince Rudolf. Death of Field-Marshal Radetzky.	
1859 Battles of Magenta and Solferino. Loss of all Lombardy. Death of Metternich.	
1862 *Johannes Brahms settles in Vienna.*	1862 Bismarck becomes Prime Minister of Prussia.
1864 *Invention of the internal combustion engine by Siegfried Marcus.*	
	1865 Murder of Abraham Lincoln. *First edition of "Alice in Wonderland".*
1866 Battles of Custozza and Lissa. Battle of Königgrätz. Loss of Venice. *Peter Mitterhofer of Tyrol invents the typewriter.*	
1867 The "Arrangement" with Hungary. *Opening of the Brenner railway.*	1867 Murder of Emperor Maximilian of Mexico. The USA acquire Alaska from Russia.
1869 *Opening of the Vienna Opera House.*	
	1870 Birth of Lenin.
	1871–90 Bismarck Chancellor of Germany.

Austria	*Elsewhere*
1872 *Death of Grillparzer.*	
1874 *Johann Strauss's "Fleder-maus".*	1874 Birth of Winston Churchill.
1875 Death of Ferdinand I in Prague (abdicated 1848).	
1882 The Triple Alliance: Austria, Germany and Italy.	1883 *Death of Richard Wagner.*
1884 *Opening of the Arlberg railway.*	1886 *Death of Franz Liszt.*
1888 *Opening of the new Vienna Burgtheater.*	
1889 Death of Crown Prince Rudolf at Mayerling: Franz Ferdinand becomes heir to the throne.	
1896 *Death of Anton Bruckner.*	
1897 *Death of Johannes Brahms.*	
1897–1907 *Gustav Mahler Director of the Vienna Opera.*	
1898 Assassination of the Empress Elisabeth.	
1899 *Death of Johann Strauss.*	
	1900 *Death of Oscar Wilde.*
	1901 Death of Queen Victoria, accession of Edward VII. *Death of Verdi.*
1903 *Death of Hugo Wolf.*	
	1904 The Anglo-French Entente Cordiale. *Death of Dvořák.*
1907 Last Meeting between Franz Joseph and Edward VII of Great Britain at Bad Ischl.	
1908 Annexation of Bosnia and Herzegovina (mandated territories since 1878).	
1911 *Richard Strauss's "Der Rosenkavalier". Death of Gustav Mahler. Arnold Schönberg propounds his "12-note" system.*	1911 Amundsen reaches the South Pole in December, and
1914–18 Murder of Franz Ferdinand at Sarajevo leads to World War I.	1912 Capt. Scott in January.
1915 Italy changes sides and declares war on Austria.	
1916 21 November: Death of Franz Joseph I.	

FRANZ JOSEPH I
by the Grace of God
KAISER von ÖSTERREICH;

König von Ungarn und Böhmen, von Dalmatien,
Kroatien, Slavonien, Galizien, Lodomerien und Illyrien;
König von Jerusalem etc.; Erzherzog von Österreich;
Großherzog von Toscana und Krakau; Herzog von
Lothringen, von Salzburg, Steyer, Kärnten, Krain und
der Bukowina; Großfürst von Siebenbürgen, Markgraf
von Mähren; Herzog von Ober- und Nieder-Schlesien,
von Modena, Parma, Piacenza und Guastalla, von
Auschwitz und Zator, von Teschen, Friaul, Ragusa und
Zara; gefürsteter Graf von Habsburg und Tirol, von
Kyburg; Görz und Gradisca; Fürst von Trient und
Brixen; Markgraf von Ober- und Nieder-Lausitz und
in Istrien; Graf von Hohenembs, Feldkirch, Bregenz,
Sonnenberg etc.; Herr von Triest, von Cattaro und auf
der windischen Mark; Grosswojwod der Wojwodschaft
Serbien etc. etc.

Invested with these resplendent titles, and with the
strong right arm of Prince Felix Schwarzenberg, his able
Prime Minister, to guide him, the young Emperor started
on his *via dolorosa* of 68 years on the throne. During all
this time, almost the only mercy he was vouchsafed was to
die just before the final crash of the dynasty and the Empire
in 1918.

The new Emperor was an absolute monarch and all that
it implies: commander-in-chief of the armed forces, the
supreme authority in all temporal matters, and the sole
architect of foreign and domestic policy. And all this at 18.
Yet he was in no way daunted by his responsibilities. He
regarded himself, and bore himself, as appointed and
charged by Destiny with the government and preservation
of his heritage. Without this sublime confidence in his

appointed mission all his personal qualities would not have seen him through. From the very first he gave evidence of intense powers of application, unwavering conscientiousness, a stern sense of duty, and a prodigious memory. In his personal relationships he was at all times correct and above all courteous to high and low alike. Among his other outstanding qualities were dignity and iron self-control, and it was this coolness and level-headedness in times of crisis that gave rise to the legend that he had no heart, no human feelings at all. On the contrary, there was an ardent emotional element in him which had to be kept very firmly in check, as will be seen in due course.

There were faults too of course, and they became increasingly evident as time went on. On the death of the invaluable Schwarzenberg in 1852 the young Emperor embarked upon an experiment in autocracy by taking everything into his own hands, and this lack of the ability to delegate, and his mistrust of anyone of outstanding ability, were to have unhappy consequences in years to come. His meticulous punctuality, utter reliability and undeviating routine are the attributes of a first-class Civil Servant, but not of a leader. A leader must have elasticity, flair and vision, and these were qualities that Franz Joseph conspicuously lacked. Nor could his seemingly unruffled calm conceal a reluctance to take decisions that at times amounted to vacillation, aggravated no doubt by a long life of failures and agonising disappointments. The fact that he was not an intellectual and knew nothing of art, music or literature was neither here nor there: what was important was that the multi-racial Empire should have as its pivot a ruler who by his personal example could hold it together, and this, for all his faults, is Franz Joseph's supreme achievement. For 68 years of almost unbroken misfortune and disaster he never swerved or flinched from the mission for which, he was convinced, Destiny had appointed him. His fortitude was almost superhuman.

Furthermore, he was a born ruler. By sheer force of example, without a spark of genius, he somehow kept the ship of State afloat through the most appalling disasters, and when he died it was still afloat. If Maximilian I was the last of the knights, Franz Joseph was the last of the monarchs, and he said as much to Theodore Roosevelt when they met in Vienna in 1910.

Within a year of his accession he was with the army in Italy under Field-Marshal Count Josef Radetzky, who in a brilliant campaign extinguished the last embers of the 1848 uprising, so that by the end of the year all the revolts of 1848 had been quelled, Lombardy and Venice were secure, Tuscany and Modena were being ruled by Habsburg princes, and the young Emperor had had his baptism of fire in the field. But just as his inheritance seemed to be settling down to a long era of peace and prosperity, the Emperor's right-hand man, Felix Schwarzenberg, died and Franz Joseph confidently embarked upon his experiment in autocracy, ruling through the triple agency of the Church, the Civil Service and the Army. The experiment was, to put it mildly, not a success, and by his policy of neutrality during the Crimean War Franz Joseph managed to antagonise half Europe, though in all fairness it is difficult to see what else he could have done. If he had sided against Russia he would have been helping the revolutionary Louis Napoleon of France and, indirectly, Prussia: if he had taken Russia's side he would have been bringing the menace of Russian expansion uncomfortably close to Austria's Balkan interests. Whatever the pros and cons of either policy, the fact remains that by failing to come to Russia's help as Russia had come to his in helping to suppress the Kossuth rising in Hungary in 1849 Franz Joseph, as well as exposing Austria's weakness to the whole of Europe, soured relations with Russia for the rest of his reign and perhaps even sowed the first seeds of World War I.

History has not been kind to Franz Joseph over this episode: but it was the system, rather than he personally, that was at fault. It should never have been possible for so young and inexperienced a ruler, however self-confident, to place himself in a position where he was the sole arbiter of the destinies of an Empire of 50 million subjects. It should never have been possible for him to experiment with absolutism on Schwarzenberg's death, but it was; and the results were catastrophic. Clearly he needed guidance; a wife, perhaps? His mother Sophie, who was an indefatigable match-maker, had been looking round the Courts of Europe for some time and had eventually turned to a branch of her own family in Bavaria. A family gathering at Ischl in Upper Austria was arranged and Franz Joseph duly obliged by falling in love — but with the wrong girl. Not only was he bowled over by the 16-year old younger sister of his "intended" but she too was swept off her feet, and before the house-party had got properly into its stride Franz Joseph was duly engaged to Elisabeth, the grand-daughter of King Maximilian I of Bavaria and therefore a Wittelsbach. Even in those early years her beauty was startling, but neither by upbringing nor by inclination was she ready for marriage, certainly not to the Emperor of Austria. But married they were, in the Augustinian Church in Vienna on 24 April 1854; and without even the relaxation of a honeymoon Elisabeth at the age of 17 was expected to play her part as Empress of Austria under the eagle eye of her forbidding mother-in-law, Franz Joseph's mother Sophie. Another impossibility. But she loved him for the time being; and he loved her all her life.

The year 1858, the tenth anniversary of Franz Joseph's accession, brought the birth of his son and heir Rudolf and the death of the aged Field-Marshal Radetzky, so that to his control of foreign affairs Franz Joseph now added the overall command of Austrian armies in the field. In the exercise of the first he was manoeuvred by King Victor Emanuel of Sardinia's brilliant Foreign Minister, Cavour, into declaring war on the combined forces of Sardinia and Louis Napoleon of France; and in the exercise of the second he suffered a moderate reverse at the Battle of Magenta and a decisive one in the appalling carnage of the Battle of Solferino (June 1859), where the dead and wounded amounted to close on 40,000. Under the terms of the ensuing peace Austria lost all Lombardy, this time for good, and the Duchies of Tuscany and Modena were also ceded to the Kingdom of Sardinia, but Austria was allowed (for the time being) to keep Venetia, in which France was not interested. Perhaps the most ominous feature of the whole disastrous campaign was that the loyalty of the Slav and Magyar regiments under fire was more than suspect, which was not surprising: one can hardly string up a country's leaders (1849) and then expect its soldiers to fight enthusiastically in a war that is none of their business.

It was therefore in a distinctly chastened mood that Franz Joseph returned to Vienna in 1860. He had lost nearly all his territories in Italy, he had mortally offended the Czar, the Hungarian pot was beginning to simmer again, and things were not going well in the home. Elisabeth was finding her mother-in-law intolerable and had even begged Franz Joseph to let her come to him in Italy and do some hospital work. He had refused, and she was now sulking. An even greater irritation was her mother-in-law's attempt to monopolise the education of the children (by now two girls as well as Rudolf). Almost frantic with frustration, Elisabeth had been spending hours on end in the saddle — anything to get away from the *ménage à trois* at Schloss Laxenburg, just south of Vienna. Three years previously she had visited Hungary, and had at once fallen in love with everything Hungarian, even to the extent of learning the fiendishly difficult language. Is it

Klemens Wenzel Lothar Prince Metternich

Crown-Prince Rudolf

fanciful to detect here an element of perversity: had she perhaps made up her mind to champion the Hungarians even before she had ever set eyes on them, simply to spite her mother-in-law, who seldom lost an opportunity of emphasising how much she detested them? The fact remains that Elisabeth for almost the last time in her life now threw herself into politics and spent most of her time among Hungarians, bombarding Franz Joseph with letters pleading their cause. By 1860, what with one thing and another, she was mentally and physically at the end of her tether, and a prolonged rest in a warmer climate was deemed imperative. Readily accepting an offer from Queen Victoria of England, she sailed from Antwerp in the royal yacht "Victoria and Albert" to Madeira and stayed there until May 1861. On her return to Vienna she at once had a relapse and was packed off again, this time to Corfu, where she remained for over a year. It was during these two periods far from home (and her mother-in-law) that she changed into a reserved, withdrawn, highly sensitive and above all mature woman, restless and for ever on the move, not so much in search of the unattainable as in flight from her own failure. Perhaps too she suffered from a taint of the instability for which the Wittelbachs were notorious. At all events from now on, with one or two brief and isolated exceptions, she hardly ever visited her husband and was very seldom seen at Court. She had to all intents and purposes abdicated from Imperial responsibilities.

Meanwhile poor Franz Joseph, as if the Hungarians were not quite enough of a handful, now found himself menaced from the north. In 1862 Prince Otto von Bismarck became Prime Minister of Prussia. Taking advantage of Austria's weakness after 1848, with a new and untried Emperor at the helm, Bismarck had been steadily advocating a policy of challenging the Austrian hegemony in the German League. Eager to repair his tarnished prestige

after the Italian disasters Franz Joseph conceived the idea
of convening the Council of German Princes at Frankfurt
in 1863 in order to demonstrate Austria's hegemony in
defiance of Prussia (and also in defiance of the pro-Prussian
policy of Metternich, who had died four years previously).
But Bismarck had other ideas. He had no intention of
allowing the Federal Diet at Frankfurt to be dominated by
Austria: what he wanted was a united Germany, a German
Empire under Prussian leadership and excluding Austria.
And if excluding Austria meant war — well, that was what
it would have to come to. His first step therefore was to
persuade the King of Prussia not to attend the Diet at
Frankfurt. In the King's absence the Council of Princes
presided over by Franz Joseph was without meaning or
purpose, and after several exhausting sessions all Franz
Joseph could do was to make his way ruefully back to
Vienna, calling en route on Queen Victoria of England,
who was staying with some of her German relatives. Both
deplored Prussia's absence from the Council and that was
all.

Bismarck now pushed ahead preparations for the exclusion of Austria from the German League by force. Whether
he needed an ally or not, circumstances presented him with
one. Italy had offered to buy Venetia from Austria for
1,000 million Lire, and Franz Joseph had refused on
altruistic grounds. So if it came to war between Austria and
Prussia and Prussia won, Italy, by joining in however
ineffectively on the Prussian side, could make sure of a
share in the spoils. When it did come in the summer of
1866 the war was short and sharp. After a try-out against
Denmark in 1864 Bismarck was confident that the Prussian
army had the beating of the Austrians and so it proved.
The superior generalship (Helmuth von Moltke) of the
Prussians and their new breech-loading rifles left the
Austrians no chance, and after the decisive battle of Königgrätz (now Hradec Králové) in Bohemia the Prussians

captured Prague and began to advance on Vienna. Before they got there Bismarck called off the chase and an armistice was agreed, and by the Peace of Prague Austria was duly excluded from the German League. In other respects the Peace Treaty was a lenient one: once he had secured Austria's exclusion from the German League it was not Bismarck's policy to humiliate or embitter her. He was looking ahead to the day when Austria (he hoped) would be his ally against France.

In the fighting against Italy Austria won the battles and lost the peace. On land, the Archduke Albrecht won a brilliant victory at Custozza, and on sea the Austrian fleet commanded by Admiral Wilhelm von Tegetthoff finished off the numerically superior Italian fleet at the extraordinary battle of Lissa by the simple but revolutionary expedient of ramming the enemy's capital ships with his· ironclads. But as Austria had lost the war against Prussia Venetia had to be given up to Prussia's ally, Italy, and that was the end, once and for all, of Austrian domination in northern Italy.

After the dust of Königgrätz had settled Austria had peace for over 40 years — until 1914.

The year 1866 was more than a military disaster for Austria — it was the beginning of the end. It was the end of the established order that Metternich had tried to build up, and it was the culminating consequence of Franz Joseph's series of vacillations, experiments and mistakes. Austria was now out of Germany and out of Italy: an implacably hostile Russia was meddling in the Balkans, and Hungary was still smouldering. Something would have to be done about Hungary very soon.

The Empress Elisabeth had come out of her shell during the war against Prussia and had thrown herself whole-heartedly into hospital and welfare work. There had been a reconciliation with Franz Joseph, and after the defeat she took the children to Budapest in view of the Prussian advance on Vienna, and there she stayed, still tirelessly plying the unfortunate Emperor with letter after letter pleading the cause of her beloved Hungarians. Negotiations with the Hungarian Ministers dragged on all through the autumn and winter of 1866 and it was not until the spring of 1867 that an agreement know as the "Ausgleich", or compromise settlement, was hammered out. From now on the Monarchy was to be known as the Dual Monarchy of Austria-Hungary, with Franz Joseph Emperor of Austria and Apostolic King of Hungary (he was ceremonially crowned in the Coronation Church in Buda the same year). It was a partnership between two independent States under a single crown, with separate Parliaments and Prime Ministers at Vienna and Budapest. Each half of the Monarchy had its own local governments and its own official language. There was no joint Imperial Parliament, but Foreign Affairs, the Army and Finance were under joint control, the three Ministers in question being appointed by the Emperor and responsible to two Delegations, each of 60 members, from the two Parliaments. The Delegations met twice a year at Vienna and Budapest alternately and communicated with each other only in writing. The Austro-Hungarian Dual Monarchy was based on the Church, the Army, the Bureaucracy and the Police, "the masses", in Wickham Steed's picturesque phrase, "being simply there to be governed". The ruling casts were the German-speaking peoples in one half of the Monarchy and the Magyars in the other.

The ingredients of the two halves were as follows:

Administered by Vienna:
Austria (with South Tyrol), Bohemia, Moravia, part of Silesia, Galicia, Bukovina, Istria (Pola and Trieste), Carniola, and Slovenia.

Peoples:	Austrians	12	million
	Czechs	6,5	million
	Poles	5	million
	Ruthenians	3,5	million
	Slovenes	1,5	million
	Serbo-Croats	0,75	million
	Italians	0,75	million
	Rumanians	0,25	million
	TOTAL	30,25	million

Administered by Budapest:

Hungary, Dalmatia, Croatia, (Fiume), Voivodina (Serbs), Transylvania (Rumanians), parts of present-day Rumania, Slovakia and Ruthenia.

Peoples:	Magyars	10	million
	Rumanians	3	million
	Slovaks	2	million
	Austrians	2	million
	Ruthenians	0,5	million
	Serbo-Croats	2,75	million
	TOTAL	20,25	million

It must be emphasised that all these races were citizens of Austria-Hungary and were scattered all over the Dual Monarchy: except for the Italians, they were not confined to any one enclave or area. Most family trees would contain members of at least three different races. By and large however the internal tension was by no means negligible; notably Magyars and Czechs against Austrians; and Serbs, Croats, Slovenes and Rumanians against Magyars. The Croats were a particulary thorny problem. Their language is akin to Serbian, but their religion is Roman-Catholic, and they marched against Hungary under Jellačić in 1848 with the greatest enthusiasm. They were doubly unfortunate in coming under Magyar domination and, because of their language, being classed as akin to the Serbs, whom they looked down upon as primitive and uncouth. Yet they were among Franz Joseph's most loyal subjects.

The "Ausgleich" might well have been the first step in the direction of a "Commonwealth" in the modern sense, but it was never followed up. The Archduke Franz Ferdinand, as will be seen, had ideas of expanding Dualism into Trialism by including the Slavs, but the Hungarians would never have countenanced such a plan; and in any event Franz Ferdinand's murder at Sarajevo in 1914 removed the last hope of any progressive modifications to the constitution. And in any case the "Ausgleich" was not an agreement between two States, but between Franz Joseph and the Hungarian nobles. The original agreement provided for amendments every ten years as occasion demanded, but the Hungarians were never honest partners and had no scruples about sabotaging the joint foreign policy and the joint economic and military measures if it suited them to do so. Nor is it an exaggeration to point to their lamentable treatment of the minorities under their rule as being a prime factor in the disintegration of the Monarchy in 1918. All in all the "Ausgleich" was very far from a solution of the perpetual nationalities problem because it only exacerbated the sullen and implacable hostility of the Slavs in both halves, and because neither of the two dominant races, the Austrians and the Magyars, represented a majority in their respective halves. Worst of all, from now on Austria's centuries-old supremacy in Europe was gone, and the Dual Monarchy was uncomfortably sandwiched between a triumphant Prussia and an emergent Italy.

All this time, plans had been steadily going ahead for making Vienna into a modern Imperial capital. On the last day of 1857 Franz Joseph had signed the decree for the razing of the old medieval bastions, and over the open expanse of *glacis* (which for defence reasons had never been allowed to be built over) between the Inner City and the 34 outer suburbs there was laid out the magnificent new Ringstrasse lined with trees and promenades and splendid new buildings on both sides: the mock-Flemish Rathaus; the neo-classical Parliament; the Renaissance University; two great Museums with a superb statue of Maria Theresia between them; a magnificent open space in front of the Hofburg (the Heldenplatz) with equestrian statues of Prince Eugene and Archduke Karl (Napoleon's conqueror at Aspern); the fine new Burg Theatre (opened in 1888) opposite the Rathaus; and on the finest site of all, where the Ringstrasse crossed the main road to Trieste and the south, the new Opera House, which was ceremonially opened on 25 May 1869 with Mozart's "Don Giovanni".

Further afield, the manifold arms into which the Danube divided just north of the city were tidied up, and the main stream diverted into its present course to obviate the danger of flooding. To the north-west the vast Vienna Woods formed a natural Green Belt, and to the east, stretching away into the distance as far as the eye could see, was the great Hungarian Plain, with the faint smudge of the Little Carpathians in the far distance. (It is only recently that Vienna has ventured to stretch out tentacles eastwards on the far side of the Danube.)

The last 30 years of the 19th century and the first 14 of the 20th were a period of unbroken peace, and it was as if the capital had decided to turn its back on all the disasters of the previous 30 years or more and emulate the great Baroque upsurge after the rout of the Turks in 1683. It was a kind of sunset glory with which all the arts and sciences were equally suffused. Johannes Brahms of Hamburg settled in Vienna in 1862 and remained there until his death in 1897. Anton Bruckner from St. Florian in Upper Austria wrote all his major works in Vienna, and towards the end of his days was awarded a "grace and favour" residence in a part of the Belvedere, where he died in 1896, a year

103

before Brahms and 7 years before Hugo Wolf. And of course it was the "Golden Age" of Viennese operetta — Suppé, Millöcker, the Strauss dynasty, and a good deal later Lehár. Then there was the decade 1897—1907, perhaps the finest in the history of the Vienna Opera, during which Gustav Mahler was Director before being edged out by constant intrigues and departing for America, disillusioned and mortally ill. He eventually returned to Vienna and died in 1911, the same year as the first performance of Richard Strauss's opera of Viennese life in the days of Maria Theresia, "Der Rosenkavalier". Among the painters the outstanding names were Gustav Klimt and Egon Schiele, both of whom died in 1918. Vienna could also boast world-famous names in the domain of medicine, notably Ignaz Semmelweis, the conqueror of puerperal fever, and Sigmund Freud, whose pioneer work in the field of psycho-analysis is part of world history. It was also an age of great progress in engineering, notably the opening of the Semmering Railway in 1854, of the Brenner railway in Tyrol in 1867, and of the Arlberg railway in 1884. Among Austrian inventions pride of place must go to Siegfried Marcus's first internal combustion engine (1864), the first typewriter (1866) constructed by Peter Mitterhofer of Tyrol, Josef Madersperger's sewing-machine, and Josef Ressel's marine propeller. Last, but by no means least, a few years after the turn of the century the new "Vienna School" in music was launched by Arnold Schönberg's "twelve-note" system of tonality, his most important disciples being Alban Berg, who died on Christmas Eve in 1935, and Anton von Webern, who was accidently shot in a temporary internment camp in 1945.

Far from being vouchsafed a period of tranquillity to recover from the disastrous consequences of his mistakes in the military and diplomatic fields, Franz Joseph was now assailed by a series of tragedies in his domestic life under which even his superhuman fortitude almost gave way.

First, there was the assassination in 1867 of Franz Joseph's younger brother Maximilian. He was married to Charlotte, the daughter of King Leopold of Belgium, who was as ambitious as Maximilian's mother Sophie but far less calculating and efficient. These two ladies were both determined that Maximilian should not be eclipsed by the glory of his Imperial brother, and it so happened that the throne of Mexico, the gift of the French Emperor, was going begging at the time. Maximilian needed no prodding: he was obsessed with visions of a sort of Eldorado Empire in the New World, and Franz Joseph's prudent advice to secure firm guarantees before embarking on what seemed to him a wild-goose chase was drowned by the adulation and enthusiasm of his wife and mother. Franz Joseph insisted that it was a crazy speculation and implored his brother to hold back, even pointing out that if anything happened to the infant Rudolf, who was by no means robust, Maximilian was the heir to the throne unless Elisabeth had another son, which was unlikely. Either Maximilian was to call off the whole escapade or the Emperor would be forced to debar him from the right of succession in Austria-Hungary. Maximilian would not be deterred, so Franz Joseph had no option but to go in person to Maximilian's castle of Miramar, just outside Trieste, to get his brother's signature to the deed of renunciation. Maximilian hurried to Mexico, encountered the violent, universal and persistent hostility of the Mexicans, and was virtually a prisoner in his palace. Charlotte then embarked on the long voyage back to Rome to implore the Pope to save the situation, but neither the Pope nor the French Emperor were disposed to intervene beyond giving Maximilian their blessings. Eventually the situation in Mexico came to a head; there was a revolution, and Maximilian was shot by a firing-squad. Charlotte, whose ghost still seems to haunt the castle of Miramar, went mad, while Sophie was at last convinced that she had shot her bolt and reluctantly but gracefully retired from the scene.

As time went on the heir to the throne, Rudolf, grew up into far more robust manhood than his precarious infancy had suggested. There was little of his father about him except his love of Army life, which was all the more strange in view of his liberal ideas and his pronounced intellectual tastes. Even more curious was his close boyhood friendship with his cousin Franz Ferdinand, next in line to the succession, with whom he had almost nothing in common. True to his practice of never delegating authority, Rudolf's father would not allow him any share in affairs of State, with the result that out of sheer frustration Rudolf, in modern parlance, got into bad company. Although (or because) there was so much more of his mother than of his father in him Elisabeth had been allowed precious little say in his upbringing; and now his father was deliberately treating him as a small boy instead of instructing him in how to run the Empire (and nobody was better qualified to do so than Franz Joseph). What with youthful impatience to claim his inheritance, and a substantial measure of congenital instability, Rudolf "went wrong". Tired of planning liberal reforms that he despaired of ever being allowed to institute (as Joseph II had been by his mother Maria Theresia); and fretting at the apparent impossibility of enjoying any sort of private life of his own at Court, he began to frequent the company of exactly the kind of freethinkers and anti-clerical intellectuals that were calculated to make his father more obstinately withdrawn than ever. Marriage did not help either: entirely against Elisabeth's advice Franz Joseph had selected for Rudolf the colourless, jejune and inadequate Princess Stephanie, a daughter of King Leopold II of Belgium, and if Rudolf ever loved her at all it was not for very long.

Now Rudolf, for all his frustration and impatience, was

106

gifted with great personal charm and was immensely popular in the Army, which was one of the two environments he was completely happy in, the other being the circles among which he preferred to find his amusements. Amusements is perhaps an understatement: his playboy, boisterous existence was more or less common knowledge in Vienna. So Rudolf continued to drown his frustration in drink and diversions, and in 1887 he felt himself constrained to take the extreme step of writing a letter to the Pope. What the letter contained will perhaps never be known for certain. One theory is that it was an appeal for his marriage to be annulled. Others maintain that it was a cri-de-cœur about all that his relations with his father ought to have been and were not, ending in an appeal for help and guidance. What is quite certain is that the letter was brought (as it was bound to be) to the attention of the Emperor, who sent for Rudolf and expressed his disappointment, to put it mildly. That was on 26 January 1889. The very next day Rudolf went off to his hunting-lodge at Mayerling in the Vienna Woods some twenty miles or so south-west of Vienna, having previously arranged, as we know, for a young friend of his, Baroness Marie Vetsera, aged 17, to meet him there. Everyone must be familiar with the outline of the story by this time: the door of the bedroom in the hunting-lodge having to be forced open next morning; the two bodies, and the unmistakable evidence that it was Marie who had been shot first, her body being covered with flowers. There were also letters in Rudolf's handwriting to his wife and his mother, but to his father he wrote nothing. And then the macabre procedure of spiriting Marie's body away before the Press got on to it: fully clothed and propped up between two uncles it was driven at dead of night through blinding rain and sleet to the nearby Monastery of Heiligenkreuz — and there buried under police supervision. As for Rudolf, he was buried in the Capuchin vault in Vienna as if it had not been suicide at all, after an altercation between the Emperor and the Cardinal-Archbishop of Vienna. Rudolf was 31 when he died.

Almost 80 years after the event, one can only marvel at the way the Court managed to hush up the details, apart of course from the material evidence. Even today the whole truth is still a matter for conjecture. That it was suicide is generally accepted: but the popular romance of a "love-pact" is only for the motion-picture industry. That Marie loved Rudolf is tolerably certain: that her love was obviously hopeless is the reason why she agreed to accompany him on his last journey. That Rudolf loved Marie is most unlikely: having determined to take his life, but lacking the courage to do so in solitude, he was only too grateful to find someone who would go with him.

The scene of the tragedy was demolished by order of the Court, and on the site of the hunting-lodge is now a Carmelite convent. It is still a favourite place to make an expedition to on a summer Sunday afternoon.

When the news of Rudolf's death reached the Vienna Hofburg Elisabeth was for once in a while in residence. But having stood by her husband at his terrible hour for them both, she was soon off again, flitting restlessly from one favourite haunt to another in search of — what? In the past she had enjoyed the hunting in England, and even more so in Ireland, but she was increasingly troubled by rheumatism and had to give up riding in 1882. Extremely indicative of her relations with Franz Joseph at this time is an extract from a letter he wrote her three years after Rudolf's death: "I should like to put into words how very, very deeply I love you, though I am not very good at showing it and it would only bore you if I did." As the 19th century drew to its close Elisabeth spent more and more of her time in her villa on the island of Corfu: there was no question of her returning to Vienna, but she made several trips to Switzerland. It was while sightseeing in Geneva on 10 September 1898 that she was fatally stabbed by an Italian anarchist while boarding one of the lake-steamers. It was a completely pointless act and it had no political consequences whatever. For the Emperor, it was surely the final blow in a seemingly endless series of disasters and tragedies: the loss of Italy, the humiliation of Königgrätz, the murder of Maximilian, the death of Rudolf, and now this? But it was not the final blow.

After the death of Rudolf the heir to the throne was the Emperor's nephew, the Archduke Franz Ferdinand, who was 26 at the time. Before he was 40 he was the Emperor's representative in the Army High Command and a full cavalry general. Since the triumph of Prussia in 1866 there had been big changes in the European political scene. Prussia had soundly beaten the French in 1870 and the German Empire, under Prussian leadership, had been proclaimed in Paris the following year. In 1878 there was a Congress at Berlin, convened on the initiative of the British Prime Minister Benjamin Disraeli, at which Austria-Hungary was invited to administer the territories of Bosnia and Herzegovina as a mandate, but nothing was said about their being annexed. The following year Bismarck set the seal upon the policy he had embarked on in 1866 by negotiating the Dual Alliance with Austria. It was a mutual defensive alliance against Russia, whose subversive Pan-Slav activities in the Balkans were regarded with growing concern in Vienna. In 1882 the Dual Alliance was expanded into the Triple Alliance by the accession of Italy, but Italy insisted on the insertion of a clause absolving her of any obligation that would involve her in hostilities against Great Britain. If Königgrätz was the beginning of the end of the Dual Monarchy, it was this Dual Alliance that, seen in retrospect, sealed its fate, for it meant that Germany was bound to support any operations, however headstrong, by Austria in the Balkans; Austria was bound to support Germany against France and Russia; and France and Russia were therefore thrown into each other's arms. The inevitable consequence of the Dual Alliance, sooner or later, was bound to be a European war, and the disintegration of the Austro-Hungarian Monarchy if it was on the losing side.

At the turn of the century however Europe was still enjoying peace and prosperity, and no one was more determined to keep the peace than Franz Joseph. Of all the Great Powers Austria had least to gain by war. And so the Emperor, well on in years now but with an amazing physical constitution, toiled away at his desk day after day, rising from his iron field-bed in Schönbrunn Palace at 4 o'clock every morning to start the long day's administrative routine in which he sought refuge from his sorrows. If he were to give way, what would happen to the Empire? Over fifty years he had held it together by his personal example: he was the sole focus of unity, and of the army's loyalty. He had made many, many mistakes, but his bearing, his fortitude had earned him universal respect; and now that he was growing old and bent under the blows of Fate the respect ripened to affection. Perhaps great age is an indispensable qualification for popularity: there is a parallel here with Queen Victoria. But Franz Joseph was an absolute, not a constitutional monarch, and as he had always refused to delegate any of his responsiblities he was indispensable. Indeed, he had once said that he doubted whether it was possible for Austria-Hungary to be governed by a Parliamentary system. Now he had become so much of an autocratic institution that the common superstition that when he died it would be the end of the Monarchy became a seriously held belief. But he must not die: Austria-Hungary without him would be inconceivable.

The summers were spent at the Imperial villa at Bad Ischl in Upper Austria, shooting, relaxing, and being visited by the younger European royalty for advice and support. Among them was King Edward VII of England, who was gifted with far greater vision and statesmanship

110

than any other monarch of his time. He brought all his diplomatic charm to bear on the old Emperor in an effort to dissuade him from the undoubtedly honourable but disastrous policy he had embarked upon at Germany's side, but to no purpose. The Emperor's obstinacy only unbended to the extent of being persuaded to be taken for a ride in a motor-car for the first and only time in his life at the age of 77. It is fascinating to speculate on what the future of Central Europe would have been if Edward VII had succeeded in unhooking Austria from Germany. If only . . .

As things were, a European clash was now to all intents and purposes inevitable: it was merely a question of when and where it would be sparked off. It was all but sparked off by Franz Joseph's announcement in 1908 that the territories of Bosnia and Herzegovina over which he had been awarded a mandate at the Berlin Congress of 1878 had now been annexed. And what was more, Austria annexed them without informing her allies, Germany and Italy. All Europe was in an uproar, and it was Germany who averted war by making no secret of her intention of standing by Austria if Russia made a move.

The annexation was the outcome of a long diplomatic tussle between Austria and Russia. Austria was anxious to contain Pan-Slavism in the Balkans, of which Serbia was regarded as the hotbed. In return for acquiescence in the annexation, Russia expected Austrian support for the opening of the Bosphorus to her shipping. Austria had also spent and invested a great deal of money in improving the standard of living in this somewhat backward corner of Europe and expected some return on her money. There was the further factor, in view of Franz Joseph's obsession with handing over his inheritance intact at his death, that Bosnia and Herzegovina represented some compensation for the loss of the Italian territories. On the other hand, he was almost equally obsessed with keeping the peace,

111

and it is difficult to see what made him run such a terrible risk of a European war by making what appeared to be a snap decision. It is not true that Franz Joseph in old age meekly signed what his Ministers put before him, for as late as 1911 we find him giving his Chief of Staff, Field-Marshal Franz Conrad von Hötzendorf, quite clearly to understand that his persistent sniping at the Foreign Minister over the question of a preventive war against Serbia would not be tolerated. "I alone am responsible for foreign policy," the Emperor went on: "foreign policy is my affair, and my policy is a policy of peace. The Foreign Minister is merely carrying out my policy."

"Alone" is the operative word. The heir to the throne, Franz Ferdinand, had as little say in policy as Rudolf had had. Kept completely out in the cold, Franz Ferdinand surrounded himself at the Belvedere (his official residence) with a sort of opposition clique not unlike the present-day "Shadow Cabinet". Two of his leading henchmen were Count Ährenthal, Foreign Minister from 1906—1912, and Franz Conrad von Hötzendorf, who was Chief of the Imperial Staff from 1906 to 1911 and again from 1912 to 1917, though Franz Ferdinand was as emphatically against the latter's "preventive war against Serbia" agitation as the Emperor was. But this was about the only point on which Franz Ferdinand and Franz Joseph were in agreement; indeed, the antipathy between them was on a par with that between Elisabeth and her mother-in-law Sophie. Where Franz Ferdinand disagreed with the Emperor most violently was on the policy to be adopted towards the Slavs in general and Serbia in particular. He was the only Habsburg who had yet formulated practical ideas of a modern, decentralised association of States on the lines of the future British Commonwealth, united by loyalty to the ruling House; or alternatively, a Federation of equal autonomous nations all owing allegiance to the Crown, with a joint central direction of finance, and of foreign and military

112

The Empress Elisabeth, by Josef Kriehuber

The Emperor Franz Joseph I

affairs, and without racial discrimination. The plan would inevitably have encountered the implacable hostility of the Hungarians as it would have involved prising over 5 million Serbs, Croats, Slovaks and Ruthenians out of Hungarian rule, and this was something the Emperor could never countenance, bound as he was by his Hungarian Coronation Oath to preserve the Hungarian domains intact. Franz Ferdinand however was not so bound, and if he had lived he would almost certainly have re-modelled the Empire on a "tripartite" basis, an equal partnership of Austrians, Slavs and Magyars. But it was not to be.

Where Franz Ferdinand was at a disadvantage, for all his statesmanlike qualities (quite apart from his admirable reforms in the Army and above all the Navy), was in what is known in modern jargon as his "public image". In appearance he was aggressive and forbidding, with fierce upturned moustaches like the German Emperor's, and bulbous eyes; and his tendency to think the worst of people until they could prove him wrong probably derived from the constant indignities he was put to through having a non-royal wife, and a Czech at that. He had had to fight a bitter battle with the Emperor to be allowed to marry her at all, and Franz Joseph only gave in with a bad grace on condition that their children were debarred from the succession. She proved an excellent wife and mother in every way but never succeeded in cutting through the icy chilliness of Court protocol.

Meanwhile the Balkans had been ravaged by two local wars, at the end of which a cock-a-hoop Serbia emerged very much on the winning side in 1913, and as confident of Russia's support in the event of any unpleasantness as Austria-Hungary was of Germany's. By a most unfortunate coincidence, but with no provocative intent, the annual Austrian summer manoeuvres had been arranged to take place in the newly-acquired Province of Bosnia, and Franz Ferdinand would be attending them in his capacity

113

of Inspector-General of the Army before paying an official visit to the local capital of Sarajevo. This was an opportunity Serbian terrorist organisations, particularly the notorious "Black Hand", had been waiting for for years. It was a pity of course that the Emperor himself was too old to make the journey, but the heir to the throne would be the next best victim. Despite repeated warnings, even from Serbian quarters, Austrian security precautions at Sarajevo were woefully inadequate. The manoeuvres were duly carried out in sweltering heat: Franz Ferdinand and his wife proceeded to Sarajevo and embarked on their ceremonial drive in an open car. On the way to the City Hall a bomb was thrown at them but missed. On the way back, after some confusion as to whether the route had or had not been changed for security reasons, both Franz Ferdinand and his wife were shot at point blank range by an assassin of the Black Hand and died within a matter of minutes. The one Habsburg who had constructive plans for the future of the Slavs had been assassinated with Serbian connivance.

The disposal of the bodies was a macabre repetition of the aftermath of Mayerling. They were brought by train to the Dalmatian coast, thence by ship to Trieste, and from there by rail to Vienna. For Franz Ferdinand, of course, there had to be a lying-in-state, but not for his non-royal wife. Knowing that permission would never be given for her to be buried with him in the Habsburg vault in Vienna, Franz Ferdinand had expressed in his will the wish that they should be buried together at his country-house at Art-stetten in Lower Austria. So the bodies had to make another train journey, and then there was the precarious crossing of the Danube in a barge on a dark and stormy night before Franz Ferdinand and his wife were at last laid to rest.

It would be appropriate at this juncture to be able to use the cliché that "events now moved rapidly to a climax".

Such however was far from the case. There were another three weeks of dithering and bickering in Vienna over what was to be done about Serbia. Conrad von Hötzendorf, who had so often claimed that the country could be wiped off the map in a matter of weeks, now began to wonder whether it was too late. The German Emperor, who in the past had more than once held Austria back from hot-headed action in the Balkans, now did precisely the opposite just when a restraining hand was most urgently required. It was Austria who was making the running now. After a great deal of diplomatic activity the Austrian Government eventually got off an ultimatum to Serbia, but not until 23 July, almost 4 weeks after the assassination. The ultimatum required Serbia's acceptance of Austria's conditions within 24 hours, or else . . . It was couched in such stiff terms as virtually to preclude any possibility of its being accepted. Yet in fact Serbia did accept 7 of the 10 points. Meanwhile however Austria had ordered a general mobilisation on 25 July, confident that the ostentatious support of the German Emperor "in shining armour", as he put it, would deter Russia from coming to the aid of her protégé Serbia. On 23 July the British Foreign Secretary Lord Grey suggested a London conference of the Foreign Ministers of Germany, France and Italy under his chairmanship, but the suggestion was turned down by Germany. And the Austrian Foreign Minister, deeming the Serbian reply inadequate, secured the Emperor's signature in his summer villa at Bad Ischl to an Austrian declaration of war on Serbia on 28 July 1914. It was the final irony in his long life that the Emperor who had so earnestly desired to keep the peace in Austria-Hungary's own interest should now be called upon to unleash a war that was to go down to history as the Great World War, a war that he did not want, was too old to direct, but could have averted. And in the very villa at Bad Ischl where King Edward VII had tried so hard to open the Austrian

Emperor's eyes to what was going to happen if he persisted in the alliance with Germany.

It has often been maintained that World War I was inevitable. So it was, once the first step had been taken. But the first step could have been avoided. Instead, it was taken — and by Austria-Hungary. After 28 July 1914 declarations of war echoed round Europe in quick succession, a chain reaction that was the inevitable result of the system of European alliances and of the impossibility of reversing mobilisations once they had got under way. On 30 July Germany declared war on Russia, and on 3 August on France. On 4 August Great Britain declared war on Germany in support of her ally, France, and on 6 August Austria-Hungary declared war on Russia. It was not until 13 August that Great Britain declared war on Austria-Hungary, and during the whole course of the war there was no clash between British and Austrian forces except towards the end on the Italian and Turkish fronts, though on the Western front Austria supplied the gigantic howitzers which so swiftly pulverised the French and Belgian fortresses.

The original belligerents were joined by Turkey in 1914 and Bulgaria in 1915 on the side of Germany and Austria-Hungary; and by Italy in May 1915, Rumania in 1916, and finally the United States on 2 April 1917 on the side of the Allies. The Italian declaration of war was in defiance of the Triple Alliance of 1882 and was the result of the Secret Treaty of London in April 1915 by which Italy was promised Trieste and all South Tyrol in return for declaring war on Austria and Germany within a month. Austrians to a man still regard it as the great betrayal, the "stab in the back".

Of all the belligerents Austria-Hungary was the only Power that had no expansionist war aims, only the chastening of Serbia and self-preservation. In fact, she had everything to lose by being towed along behind the German war-chariot and thereby becoming involved against Great Britain for no reason at all. Russia had her eyes on Constantinople, Serbia on a South-Slav Kingdom, and Rumania on the lovely land of Transylvania, then part of Hungary.

Except for the opening months, the war was fought out well beyond the Austro-Hungarian frontiers. On the Russian front hostilities were on a gigantic scale. Vast armies were locked in tremendous battles of which history has recorded a good deal less than the stories many an Austrian family can tell. In 1915 the defection of Italy meant that the Austro-Hungarian army had to fight on two fronts. Its multi-racial composition (25% German-speaking, 23% Hungarian, 44% Slav) meant that care had to be taken to keep Slav regiments on the Italian front, where they fought with the utmost tenacity, whereas on the Russian front they had found themselves fighting an enemy to whom they were more akin than they were to the side they were fighting on. Yet for all its assortment of races, this army held together for four long years on three or more different fronts, including the brief and brilliant campaign of 1916 in which Rumania was rolled up in a matter of weeks. As 1916 drew to a close the situation on the Austro-Hungarian fronts had been more than stabilised. On the evening of 20 November 1916 the Emperor, now 86 years old, retired to bed rather earlier than usual, giving instructions that he was to be called at 3.30 the next morning as "there is so much to be done". But by that time he was dead.

CHAPTER SEVEN

The Emperor Karl, the end of World War I, and the end of the Monarchy

---

Austria

Elsewhere

1916–18 Karl I of Austria-Hungary.

1917 October: The Battle of Caporetto.
December 7: The U.S.A. declare war on Austria-Hungary.
December: Rumania is knocked out of the war.

1918 March: Peace of Brest-Litovsk with Russia.
September: Collapse of the Bulgarian front.
October 28: Proclamation of the Czechoslovak Republic in Prague.
October: Collapse of the Austrian front in Italy and armistice.
November 3: Proclamation of Republic of Poland.
November 11: The Emperor Karl renounces participation in government.
November 12: Proclamation of the First Republic of Austria.
November 16: Proclamation of the Republic of Hungary.
December 1: Proclamation of the Kingdom of Yugoslavia.
Death of the painters Gustav Klimt and Egon Schiele.

1918–20 Sucessful defence of Carinthia against Yugoslav inroads.

1917 March: First Russian Revolution.
April 2: The U.S.A. declare war on Germany.
November: Second Russian Revolution under the leadership of Lenin.

1918 President Wilson's Fourteen Points.

July: The last of the Romanoff dynasty wiped out at Ekaterinburg.

November: End of World War I.

Austria	Elsewhere
1918–20 Dr. Karl Renner first Chancellor of the Republic of Austria.	
1919 March 24: The ex-Imperial family are escorted into exile in Switzerland. April 2: Habsburgs banished from Austria and property confiscated. September 16: Treaty of St. Germain. *Richard Strauss director of the Vienna State Opera.*	1919 Bela Kun's Communist regime in Hungary overthrown by Admiral Horthy, who becomes Regent. Capt. John Alcock and Lt. Arthur Brown make the first non-stop air crossing of the Atlantic. Treaty of Versailles.
1920 Plebiscite in Carinthia favours remaining with Austria. Austria a member of the League of Nations. *The first Salzburg Festival.*	
1921 Burgenland (without Sopron) accedes to Austria.	1921 April and October: two abortive attempts by ex-Emperor Karl to return to the throne of Hungary.
	1922 Death of the ex-Emperor Karl in Madeira. *Formation of the British Broadcasting Company.* Mussolini's "fascisti" march on Rome.

The death of the old Emperor was not the end, either of the empire, or of the dynasty or of the war.

The new emperor Karl, a great-nephew of Franz Joseph, was 29 years of age and had married in 1911 Zita of Bourbon-Parma. He was crowned in Budapest, but never in Vienna, and though he had commanded an army on the Russian front he had little political experience, having been pitchforked into the succession by the murder of Franz Ferdinand in 1914; but he was fortunate in enjoying the loyal support of many of the members of Franz Ferdinand's former "Belvedere" group, whose ideas the new Emperor found himself largely in sympathy with.

Karl's first concern was to withdraw Austria-Hungary from the war on the most favourable conditions obtainable, and to this end he opened secret negotiations for a separate peace through his brother-in-law Prince Sixtus of Bourbon-Parma, an officer in the Belgian army. He offered to do all he could to persuade Germany to return Alsace-Lorraine to France, and declared that Austria-Hungary had no aspirations beyond self-preservation and stopping the slaughter as soon as possible. Any hope of his offer being accepted by the Entente foundered on the relentless opposition of the Italians, who were not going to be baulked of the booty they had been promised in the secret Treaty of London, namely South Tyrol and Trieste. On the Austrian side, Hungarian resistance to any change in the constitution of the Monarchy was another insurmountable obstacle. The net result of Karl's well-intentioned but somewhat naive peace feelers was a summons to the German Emperor's headquarters at Spa in Belgium, where he was called upon to sign a document promising his Empire's unconditional adherence to Germany's conduct of the war. From now until the end of the war, Austria-Hungary was little more than a satellite of Germany.

And so the war dragged on. The people of Austria were beginning to feel the pinch of hunger too, as Hungary had drastically reduced supplies of wheat, etc. At the fronts, the situation was appreciably eased by the Russian steam-roller gradually grinding to a halt. The revolution that had been simmering in Russia for so long boiled over in March 1917, and with the arrival in Russia of Lenin (specially imported from Switzerland by the German High Command) the "October Revolution" took Russia out of the war altogether, though Russian resistance at the front had been negligible since July. But the peace negotiations with Russia were protracted by the stubborn rearguard haggling of Trotsky, and it was not until March 1918 that the Treaty of Brest-Litovsk was signed, releasing a number of Austro-Hungarian regiments for transfer to the Italian front.

Here events at last took a decisive turn towards the end of 1917. After no fewer than 11 battles along the river Isonzo near Gorizia had ended in stalemate, a gigantic Austro-Hungarian offensive, with German support, was mounted in October 1917: the Italian front was torn open at Caporetto, north of Gorizia, and the Italian armies reeled back in disorder while Austrian and German forces poured through the gap. Ernest Hemingway's marvellous "Farewell to Arms" gives a wonderfully vivid account of the confusion behind the Italian lines. It seemed as if nothing could avert the complete collapse of the entire Italian front, but as on the Marne in 1914, so now; somehow or other the miracle came to pass. British and French reinforcements were rushed from the hard-pressed Western Front, and the Italian front was eventually stabilised along the river Piave, but only after the Austrian armies had overrun a vast area of north-eastern Italy. The Austrian and German armies followed up this success by a series of mopping-up operations in Rumania which led to the elimination of Rumania from the ranks of the Entente Powers, but it was to be the last success of any significance that Germany and Austria were to be vouchsafed. The entry of the United States into the war was now beginning to affect the balance of manpower, not to mention morale, and the failure of the last desperate German offensive on the Western Front from March-June 1918 put new heart into the Italians, especially as British and French reinforcements had swollen from a trickle to a flood. The collapse of the Bulgarian front in September 1918 meant that the whole Austrian position in the Balkans was no longer tenable, and by October the last Austro-Hungarian front in Italy was beginning to crumble too. By now it was only a question of time: one by one the Slav regiments melted away, while the Hungarian regiments had already been withdrawn "for the defence of their country". So the great Austro-Hungarian army that had held together on three, and sometimes four, fronts for over four years, and kept the front line well inside enemy territory, simply disintegrated. It was perhaps the only instance in history of an army that went off to war and never came back.

Politically too the disintegration of the Empire, once it had started, spread like wild-fire. On 28 October the Czechoslovaks proclaimed a Republic in Prague, followed on 3 November by the Poles and on 16 November by the Hungarians. On 1 December came the proclamation of the Kingdom of Yugoslavia, of some 13 million Serbs, Croats and Slovenes, comprising Serbia and the former Austro-Hungarian territories of Croatia, Slovenia, Dalmatia, Bosnia, Herzegovina and Montenegro.

In Vienna, the Emperor and his advisors were left with no option but to secure the best terms they could from the victorious Entente. On the same day as the Czechoslovak Republic was proclaimed in Prague Karl wrote to President Wilson:

"The Austrian-Hungarian Government declares its readiness, irrespective of the outcome of negotiations elsewhere, to enter into negotiations for peace and an immediate armistic on all fronts."

As far back as January 1918, President Wilson had issued his famous Fourteen Points, those particularly applicable to Austria being (in brief):

Point 9. The re-adjustment of Italy's frontiers on the lines of nationality.
Point 10. The peoples of Austria-Hungary to be accorded every opportunity of autonomous development.
Point 11. Rumania, Serbia and Montenegro to be evacuated and Serbia to be given access to the sea.

Austria-Hungary
1867–1918

Austria and the
Successor States after
the Treaty of St. Germain

And of course there was the President's advocacy of "self-determination".

On 30 October a State Council was set up in Vienna with Karl Renner (of whom more will be heard in due course) as "State Chancellor". For six weeks there was the quaint situation of two different Governments in simultaneous session, the new "State Council" and the Imperial Government which had still not resigned and continued in office until 11 November when the final step was taken of requesting the Emperor to withdraw from participation in the conduct of affairs. From Schönbrunn Palace Karl thereupon issued a statement of renunciation:

"Now as ever filled with unalterable affection for all my peoples, I will not let my person be a hindrance to their free development. The people through their representatives have taken over the government. I hereby renounce all part in conducting the business of the State."

Note that it was a renunciation, not an abdication. With his family the Emperor moved from Schönbrunn Palace to a Habsburg hunting-lodge at Eckartsau on the Marchfeld east of Vienna. Four months later, as he still could not bring himself to abdicate, the State Council decreed all Habsburg property confiscated and ordered the Imperial family to quit Austrian territory, with the exception of those members of it who were prepared to renounce all their rights except those of a private citizen: those who agreed to do so could, and did, continue to live unmolested in Austria. On 24 March 1919 the ex-Imperial family travelled under British escort to Switzerland, where they were granted political asylum on condition that they engaged in no political activities. By a singular coincidence, the Habsburgs' last residence on Austrian soil, Eckartsau, is within a kilometre or two of where Rudolf, the founder of the dynasty, fought his decisive

124

battle in 1278. As the last ruling sovereign of the ancient Imperial dynasty embarked upon his last journey on Austrian soil, it may well be that the coincidence was not lost upon him.

Karl's remaining years were a grotesque and futile anti-climax. In 1921 he made two abortive attempts, in April and October, to reclaim the Crown of Hungary, Hungary (unlike Austria) having been declared a Monarchy, with Admiral Horthy as Regent, after the overthrow of the brief and bloody Communist regime of Bela Kun. It was after the second of these two escapades, on which Karl and his followers actually got within measurable distance of Budapest before being turned back, that the Swiss authorites refused to extend his political asylum on the grounds that he had broken his promise not to engage in political activities, let alone adventures. Enquiries revealed that Portugal was the only European country that was prepared to shelter him. It was on a British ship that the ex-Imperial family were conveyed to Madeira, and it was on this island, far away from his inheritance, that on 1 April 1928, after six months of desperately trying to make ends meet without any regular financial resources, the last of the Habsburg Emperors died, aged only 35.

History has neither been kind nor perhaps quite fair to Karl: he has been reproached in some quarters for being prone to acting impulsively, sometimes without too much regard for promises and undertakings solemnly entered into. In his favour let it be said that, even more so than Franz Joseph, he was placed in an impossible position. Before he had time to initiate his plans for the reform of the Monarchy, the crash came and the whole edifice fell in ruins. If nothing succeeds like success, the converse is also true: the main reason why the Monarchy disintegrated was that it was on the losing side in the Great War. It was also a victim of self-determination, though given time a solution to the nationalities' problem might well have been worked out along Commonwealth lines. But that is another story.

The immediate problems were to get the new half-fledged Republic on its feet, to alleviate hunger, and to preserve what was left of the national territory after the Succession States (Czechoslovakia, Yugoslavia and Poland) had helped themselves, not to mention Italian rapacity in seizing all South Tyrol up to the Brenner Pass. Curiously enough, in view of Tyrol's "finest hour" in 1809, the inhabitants of South Tyrol offered no resistance, whereas in Carinthia, where the Yugoslavs had surged through the Karawanken passes and even occupied Klagenfurt, the population organised a massive and systematic resistance on their own initiative and eventually succeeded in getting their claims recognised by the new League of Nations. A plebiscite was ordered, and although much of the territory in which it was held was still under Yugoslav administration, it resulted on 28 October 1920 in 59% of the inhabitants opting to remain with Austria, the Karawanken range forming the Province's natural southern frontier. Further east, in southern Styria, local resistance to Yugoslav inroads was little more than sporadic, and a large area was lost to Yugoslavia.

An Austrian delegation headed by State Chancellor Karl Renner arrived in Paris on 14 May 1919 to be handed by M. Clemenceau, the leader of the Entente representatives, the terms of a draft Peace Treaty. It was only after lengthy negotiations culminating in an Allied ultimatum that the Peace of St. Germain was eventually signed on 10 September 1919. The Successor States were represented at the Conference Table among the Allies, and Hungary was being treated separately as an independent State. Austria was alone. Under the terms of the Treaty South Tyrol, Istria, Trieste and Gorizia were ceded to Italy; and the frontiers of the Succession States were confirmed. The oil-fields of Galicia and the coal-fields of Silesia went to Poland, and the heavy industry of Bohemia and Moravia to Czechoslovakia. All that was left of the vast, self-supporting economic unit of the former Dual Monarchy were the parts that nobody else laid a claim to; or as Clemenceau put it, "l'Autriche c'est ce qui reste".

The Treaty of St. Germain also contained amongst others a clause that

> "The Allied Governments declare, and Austria agrees, that Austria and her allies are responsible for all war damage suffered by the Allies and their associates in the war forced upon them by Austria-Hungary's and her allies' act of aggression."

In other words, the Reparations Clauses imposed (theoretically) the burden of paying reparations for the whole of the former Austro-Hungarian Monarchy on the two truncated States of Austria and Hungary, a proposal that Winston Churchill later castigated as "pure nonsense".

The one solitary crumb of comfort that Austria derived from the Treaty of St. Germain was the award of a long north-south strip of former Hungarian territory south-east of Vienna, about 1,530 square miles in area. The agricultural potential of the new Province of Burgenland, hitherto under-exploited, was later to play an important part as Vienna's market-garden in keeping the capital from starvation. By manipulating a local plebiscite however Hungary retained the capital of the Province, Sopron, so that all the Province's roads and railways had to be diverted to serve the newly designated Provincial capital of Eisenstadt. Still, the new child was a welcome addition to the family of nine Provinces with which the new Austrian Federal Republic shyly took its place in the new Europe brought into being by the Peace Treaties and guaranteed by the Covenant of the League of Nations.

CHAPTER EIGHT

The First Austrian Republic, 1918—38

Austria	*Elsewhere*
1918–21 Karl Renner "State Chancellor".	
1922–24 and 1926–29 } Monsignor Ignaz Seipel Chancellor.	
1922 Austra is granted a League of Nations loan of £ 30 million.	1923 First Labour Government in Britain under Ramsay Macdonald.
	Death of Lenin, who is succeeded by Stalin.
1925 Death of Conrad von Hötzendorf. Stabilisation of the currency and introduction of the Schilling.	
1927 Riot in Vienna: burning of the Palace of Justice.	1927 *First full-length talking-film.*
1929 *Death of Hugo von Hofmannsthal.*	1929 *First Micky Mouse film.* The great slump on Wall Street. Death of Clemenceau.
1931 Collapse of the Credit-anstalt Bank.	
1932 Death of Monsignor Seipel: Dollfuss becomes Chancellor.	1929–33 Herbert Hoover President of the U.S.A.
1933 Triple Alliance Austria-Hungary-Italy.	1933 Franklin D. Roosevelt President of the U.S.A.
	Abolition of prohibition.
1934 February: Civil War in Austria. May: Dollfuss abolishes the Republic and declares a Christian Federal State. Formation of Fatherland Front.	Adolf Hitler becomes Chancellor in Germany.

Austria	*Elsewhere*
1934 July: Dollfuss murdered by Nazi terrorists. Is succeeded as Chancellor by Kurt Schuschnigg.	
1935 The Heimwehr dissolved. *Opening of the Grossglockner road.* *Death of Alban Berg.*	1935 *Death of Lawrence of Arabia.* Mussolini orders Italian annexation of Abyssinia by force.
1936 Political agreement with Germany.	1936 Death of King George V of England and accession of Edward VIII (January). Hitler re-occupies the Rhineland. Civil War in Spain until 1939. Abdication of King Edward VIII (December).
	1937 Coronation of King George VI. Neville Chamberlain becomes British Prime Minister.
1938 Schuschnigg is forced to resign as Austria is invaded by Nazi forces. Hitler in Vienna. *Oskar Kokoschka settles in England.*	1938 September: The Munich Agreement.
1939 *Death in London of Sigmund Freud.*	1939 March: Hitler occupies Czechoslovakia. August: Hitler's non-aggression pact with Stalin. September: Hitler invades Poland and starts World War II.

It was one thing to get the First Republic safely launched, but quite a different matter to keep it afloat. The first and most urgent problem was an economic one, how to stave off starvation, especially in the capital, which harboured over one-quarter of the entire population of the new Republic. The armies had disintegrated, but of the ex-soldiers who were wending their way back to Austria the majority made for the capital, so aggravating an already desperate food and housing situation. Ex-officers had to wear their uniforms because they had nothing else to wear, but the uniforms were shorn of all badges and decorations. Apart from the soldiers, there was a steady influx of Civil Servants, etc. whose jobs in the Succession States had come to an end, all instinctively flocking to what had been the great Imperial capital but was now a sort of gorified but bedraggled rehabilitation centre teeming with refugees from the four corners of the Empire. The scramble for jobs was ruthless. Imperial Civil Servants became firemen, barons became bar-pianists, and colonels became innkeepers. And by 1921 the inflation was so out of hand that wages paid out in the morning were worthless by sundown.

In the countryside bands of young men and girls wandered about the valleys begging for food and hoping for something to turn up. In Vienna the Hoover Relief Organisation from the United States worked wonders, and so did the Quakers, Schönbrunn Palace being taken over as a Welfare Centre. Austria was being kept alive by charity, from hand to mouth.

Gradually from all this misery and chaos a semblance of order was restored, and a situation developed where two main parties shared power between them: the Social Democrats, who were strongest in Vienna, and the Christian-Socials, whose strength lay in the Provinces and who within two years of the founding of the Republic were the majority party up till the suspension of the

Constitution in 1934. Politically, there seemed to be three courses open to Austria if she was to survive:

(1) A Danubian Federation.
(2) Anschluss with Germany.
(3) Restoration of the Habsburg monarchy.

The third course can be dismissed in a few lines. In 1919, whatever the Austrians themselves may have thought about it, a restoration of the monarchy would have been immediately opposed by Czechoslovakia and Yugoslavia, probably by force of arms. The ex-Emperor Karl seems to have appreciated the position fairly accurately, for his two attempts to regain his throne (both of which ended ignominiously) were directed at the Hungarian crown, not at the Austrian.

What about the first alternative, a Danubian Federation? As in the case of the monarchy, this was an expedient that was never seriously entertained because whenever the idea was launched it was immediately wrecked upon the sandbanks of suspicion in the Successor States, Czechoslovakia, Hungary, Yugoslavia, and to a lesser extent Rumania and Poland, who considered, quite reasonably, that a so-called Danubian Federation would be merely a reconstitution of the old Empire in a different form, which was certainly not what they had been fighting for. Secondly, whereas Prague, for instance, was in process of becoming a centre of trade and finance in Central Europe, a Danubian Federation would inevitably have meant that her position would have to be surrendered to Vienna, for geographical reasons if for no other. Thirdly, a Danubian Federation would have needed a strong centre, which at that time did not exist.

There remained the second alternative, Anschluss with Germany — and here one must be quite clear what is meant by Anschluss. In those days it meant quite simply union with Germany, Republican Germany. Later, of course, it meant union with Nazi Germany, in much the same way as one might talk of an Anschluss between a cat and a mouse. But in 1919 different parties interpreted Anschluss in different ways. To the Catholics, for instance, it meant one German country with a large Catholic counterpoise to the Lutheran north, while the Liberals saw in it a union against monarchy and Catholicism. The Social Democrats hoped it meant a Union under a socialist, parliamentary democratic republic and prounounced themselves in favour of it as they had no confidence in the viability of an Austrian Republic with no visible means of support. To the Pan-Germans it promised a Union with a Nationalist Greater Prussia. Finally, the Nazis later on tried to obliterate all these various conceptions of Anschluss in their demand for the unconditional fusion and subordination of Austria to the Nazi State. Yet oddly enough the Anschluss which was eventually accomplished in 1938 was none of these things: it was merely the rape of Austria by the Nazis, backed by brute force. Even the Austrian Nazis had not bargained for quite this — they had hoped by preserving a semblance of Austrian independence to secure the best pickings for themselves.

The Constitution which eventually emerged in 1922 was rather a complicated one — Austria was to be a Federal Republic of 9 provinces each with its own Diet: Upper Austria, Lower Austria, the City of Vienna, Styria, Burgenland, Carinthia, Salzburg, Tyrol and Vorarlberg. The Government was in the hands of the Christian-Socials, and for the next four years it devoted itself to the task of holding the country together, stabilising the currency, negotiating foreign credits, and maintaining internal order. That Austria was kept alive at all in the early 1920's was due very largely to the efforts of her Chancellor. Monsignor Ignaz Seipel was a remarkable figure. Throughout his career he was a practising priest and his appearance was as austere and ascetic as his way of life. He used to occupy two rooms in a Dominican Convent furnished with a table, a chair and a praying desk, and the nuns brought him his food on a plain iron dish. His usual method of transport was a tram, and he used to outrage his entourage by travelling to Geneva 2nd class. By his personal exertions he negotiated a loan from the League of Nations of £ 30 million in 1922, and by his adroit diplomacy he kept an uneasy peace between the rival political armies which were beginning to appear in Austria. He also succeeded in curbing the inflation and stabilising the currency, substituting the Schilling for the old Imperial Krone.

As for the Socialist Municipality of Vienna, its finest achievement was its housing scheme. In ten years no fewer than 60,000 flats were available to the workers in enormous tenement blocks in which a working-class family could have a flat for the equivalent of 7/- a month (about 3% of the average wage). In addition there was a housing tax of 9d. a month. The rent included cleaning and Concierge but not heat or laundry. There were no baths in the flats but the bath-house in the basement provided a bath for 5d. Other amenities were central heating, courtyard gardens, roof gardens, balconies and special playgrounds for children.

It may well be wondered how bankrupt Vienna could afford to produce this Earthly Paradise? The answer was, by placing enormous contracts (i. e. bulk purchase), by the employment of whole-time architects and engineers on a permanent salary, and by levying a multitude of small (and irritating) taxes. The actual cost to the Government of building a block containing 1700 flats was about £ 730,000. In addition to this signal contribution towards a solution of the housing problem the Municipality took energetic measures to improve the health of the children. Infant mortality, especially from tuberculosis, was very high, so special sanatoriums and health-centres for children were built in the hills around Vienna, and after 1924 the death-rate declined sharply.

By 1927 Austria had more or less settled down to Parliamentary Government under the wise guidance of Seipel, and several of the worst problems had been dealt with. But it was in 1927 that internal order began to be seriously threatened by the growth of two rival political armies, the Heimwehr and the Schutzbund: the former anti-Socialist, the latter pro-Socialist. The Heimwehr was the more formidable organisation of the two. It was started in 1919 in Carinthia as a sort of Home Guard to protect the frontier against the marauding bands of Yugoslavs in the Villach area. Soon another Heimwehr was formed in Tyrol as a protection against Italy, and later on there was also a local Heimwehr in Styria. With the easing of danger from abroad the Heimwehr became increasingly anti-Socialist. Backed by the middle classes and the Christian-Socials, it constituted itself as a defence against an imaginary Bolshevik menace. The riots of 1927, when a Socialist mob burned the Vienna Law Courts down, offered the Heimwehr an opportunity for retaliation of which it took full advantage, and by skilful propaganda it exploited these riots to gain recruits. By 1928 the Heimwehr was deliberately staging provocative demonstrations in Socialist strongholds such as Wiener Neustadt, and these clashes with the Schutzbund increased in violence and frequency when Fürst Rüdiger Starhemberg at last manoeuvred himself into the leadership, first of the Heimwehr detachment at Linz, and by 1931 of the entire organisation.

This Fürst Starhemberg was a member of an aristocratic Austrian family, impulsive and unstable, with a gift for leadership which unfortunately was not tempered by discretion. Always anti-Socialist, he later became an ardent supporter of Mussolini's Fascism, and while Italy was still strong enough to have a say in Austrian affairs he was usually assured of a place in the Government. By 1930 Heimwehr representatives were firmly established in the Government, and almost immediately a treaty of friendship was signed between Austria and Mussolini, who only a short time previously had been referring to Austria as "a miserable spittoon".

By the end of 1930, then, the future was by no means unpromising. The Heimwehr was for the moment maintaining internal order, as it had the firm support of Italy, and thanks to Chancellor Seipel Austria's credit with the League of Nations stood high. But storm-clouds were gathering on the northern horizon. Unnoticed by many the Nazis in Germany had been steadily growing in strength until in this year 1930 Hitler secured 6 million votes in the German elections. Nazi disturbances began to break out all over Austria and there was a clamour for Anschluss. Next year a Customs Union was actually agreed upon between Austria and the German *Republic*, but when the proposal was brought before the League of Nations it was strenuously opposed by France and was eventually defeated by *one* vote (the vote perhaps of some small South or Central American Republic!).

Austria is often unkindly blamed for starting the great world recession of 1931. The accusation is unfounded, but it is quite true that the first European bank failure was in Austria: the collapse of the Creditanstalt Bank in 1931. Once again, with the whole financial structure of Austria in peril, Seipel came to the rescue and organised foreign loans, including one of 50 million Schillings from Great Britain. In return, Austria had to put up with the indignity of a resident League of Nations financier in Vienna to supervise the national budget.

In 1932 Monsignor Seipel died. Economically he had steered Austria into calm waters, but other forces were massing against her, and almost exactly at the same time as Engelbert Dollfuss succeeded Seipel as Chancellor, the

Styrian Heimwehr announced that in future it looked to Adolf Hitler as its leader. It was against this sombre background that the new Chancellor took office.

It was only two years after 1930, yet the political future of Austria could hardly have seemed less inviting. In Parliament all parties were at loggerheads; the neighbouring States were erecting prohibitive tariff walls; and over all lowered the Nazi menace. Nazi threats were becoming increasingly insistent, and Nazi propaganda caused many Austrians to waver. Perhaps it was all true, perhaps Germany *was* a land flowing with milk and honey, with an assured future and no unemployment. Whereas here in Austria were bands of young people wandering aimlessly about begging substistence or inciting to disorder. Besides, the Nazis didn't ask much. "We don't want brains," they said, "all we want is your obedience." Soon the Nazis were working with all the cloak-and-dagger methods of a Secret Society. They were organised in tiny cells, a few individuals connected with a sub-leader whose name they never knew. The sub-leaders were in turn grouped under an unknown Chief who took his orders from Munich. From Germany were smuggled funds, arms, and bombs that easily eluded the Heimwehr frontier guards who had the impossible task of watching every mountain track along a 200 mile frontier.

By 1933 things had come to such a pass that Dollfuss decided upon the drastic step of dissolving Parliament. He may have been actuated in this decision by the fact that when he took over in 1932 he enjoyed a majority of one, and even that was with the assistance of Heimwehr representatives in the Government. Indeed, the increasing menace of Hitler forced Dollfuss more and more into the arms of the Heimwehr, and the Heimwehr in turn into the arms of Italy. And the Heimwehr leader Fürst Starhemberg, ardently pro-Fascist, was confident that he could rely on Italian support against Germany, for by this time Mussolini too was casting an uneasy eye north-wards over the Brenner.

Accordingly Mussolini attempted to negotiate with Hitler about the future of Austria, making him an offer which Hitler would have done well to accept. "I recognise," said Mussolini, "that Austria shall be an independent state, assimilated to Germany. My only condition is that the illegal Nazi bands in Austria are to be broken up and the Heimwehr is to be the sole legal armed force of Austria." In making this offer Mussolini felt confident that the Heimwehr was in his pocket.

Why Hitler turned this offer down remains a mystery, for in fact the Heimwehr in some parts of the country was Nazi, not Fascist. In Tyrol, for instance, any Italian invader would have met with a hot reception, while in Salzburg the Heimwehr leader was Goering's brother-in-law! But Hitler was not content, and as before in his career he preferred to stick by the old Nazi front-line fighters.

At this juncture Dollfuss very wisely paid a visit to Mussolini. Remember that at this time, 1933, Mussolini was a good deal more powerful than Hitler. Mussolini and Dollfuss immediately became firm friends and in due course a Triple Alliance of Austria, Italy and Hungary was formed with the object of making Italian ports such as Trieste available for Austrian and Hungarian exports. The benefits to the Austrian economy were obvious and Dollfuss's very sincere friendship with Mussolini was to have important consequences the following year.

But Hitler was not taking all this lying down; the great plan was slowly unfolding itself. Inexorably the pressure was kept up. Infuriated by Dollfuss's resistance and success with Mussolini, Hitler countered with a shrewd blow at one of Austria's most vital sources of income — the tourist traffic. He imposed a fee of 1000 Marks (£ 50) for visas to travel to Austria, thereby ruining the normal summer tourist traffic in the whole of Western Austria.

The Austrian Government had to subsidise the hotel industry to the extent of 10 million schillings to keep it going.

At the same time the Nazi terror inside Austria continued. Bomb outrages became increasingly frequent. Mysterious forest fires broke out at night, with the flames by some queer coincidence clearing the forests in the shape of a large Swastika. It is estimated that the Nazis in Austria by this time had grown from 3000 in 1930 to 40,000 in 1933. There was also a compact, well-drilled, fighting force of 25,000 men known as the Austrian Legion, which was kept permanently on the German side of the frontier, whence it carried out periodic terrorist raids into Austria.

The year 1933 culminated in a Nazi attempt to assassinate Dollfuss. The attempt was a clumsy one and the little man was only slightly wounded, but it provoked a storm of indignation throughout civilised Europe, and, for once, swift action inside Austria: at least 1200 Nazis were arrested and sent to prison.

And so to the year 1934, in which Austria (and indeed Europe) was twice shaken to its foundations. The year opened in an atmosphere of tension, with the Socialists, furious at the dissolution of Parliament, organising their Schutzbund into a force capable of giving the Heimwehr a good battle. To give the Socialists their due, they had honestly tried by negotiations to heal the growing breach between themselves and the Dollfuss Government. They saw clearly that unless there was a united front against the Nazis all was lost. Whether or not Dollfuss refused to negotiate with the Socialists is debatable; looking back on the events of 1934 one can see clearly that it was the lack of national unity that made Hitler a present of Austria. It is at any rate quite certain that the Heimwehr, on whom Dollfuss depended for support, would never have allowed him to negotiate with the Socialists on any terms whatever, for it was on Heimwehr insistence that Dollfuss had

138

ordered the disbandment of the Schutzbund the year before, but it was a half-hearted measure and not rigidly enforced.

By February the atmosphere was explosive. The Vienna Socialists, against the advice of their leaders, organised a general strike, and one dreary February morning in Vienna all the lights went out, all the trams stopped and all the gas was cut off. By some chance Dollfuss was in Budapest at the time and had left one of his deputies, Major Emil Fey, in charge. Fey saw his chance and took it. Determined to stamp out his arch-enemies the Socialists once and for all he mobilised the Vienna Heimwehr and flung them against the Socialist Schutzbund. There was Civil War all over Vienna. By the evening the Government had moved field artillery into Vienna and had succeeded in driving the Socialist Schutzbund into the northern part of the city, where they barricaded themselves into the huge tenement blocks which the Municipality had built ten years before. These made admirable fortresses and only after 24 hours of artillery shelling did the Socialists surrender. A bitter resistance in Floridsdorf across the Danube actually held out a little longer, but in two days it was all over. The Socialist leaders escaped to Czechoslovakia: the Mayor of Vienna was imprisoned, and the Socialist Municipality of Vienna, which had lasted since 1918, was extinguished. The exultant Heimwehr claimed the lion's share in the victory and Fürst Starhemberg for the first time used the phrase "Austro-Fascist".

It is difficult to exaggerate the shock with which the European democracies followed these events. Civil War in Vienna? Impossible. Austrians aren't like that. The cause of Austria and of Dollfuss suffered irreparable damage abroad, and Dollfuss was never forgiven by the democracies, while Dollfuss in his turn never forgave Fey for acting so ruthlessly in his absence. Only the Nazis rejoiced.

With the Socialists disposed of the way was clear for a new Constitution, and this was duly announced on 1 May 1934. Henceforth Austria was to be a Christian Federal State, and to ensure national unity Dollfuss evolved the Fatherland Front (V. F.), a non- political patriotic organisation open to all.

By June 1934 life in Vienna was gayer than at any time since 1918. The menace of nation-wide Civil War had been removed, while negotiations with Hitler had produced a statement from him that he recognised complete Austrian independence and was determined to respect it, an undertaking which the Austrian Government trusted implicitly. It almost seemed as if Vienna was its old self again. The old Imperial uniforms appeared again, a little dusty and faded perhaps, but still impressive. The brilliant Opera Ball was revived, and attended in uniform by everybody who had one. Something of the glamour and security of old Vienna had come to life again and the people were happy. Trade was good; the currency was stable; even the chronic unemployment seemed to be abating. Dollfuss had apparently performed the miracle.

It was the last supreme gesture. By July the familiar Nazi rumblings could be heard again beyond the frontier, and soon the same sickening Nazi technique was once more at work all over Austria. What did it matter to Hitler that he had promised to respect Austrian independence? Dollfuss had defied him and defied him successfully; Dollfuss must be eliminated. Rumours of an impending "putsch" began to circulate in Vienna — well, that was nothing new. But this seemed to be something different, something bigger. The anti-Austrian broadcasts from Munich were being hotted up to boiling-point and Nazi disorders were seething to a climax all over Austria. At last came the signal from Germany: "A Communist revolt is imminent in Austria, the Dollfuss Government refuses to suppress it, so we will do so." (Looking back, this was the familiar Nazi pattern of infiltration and conquest, only in 1934 it was new — Austria was the first victim.) Details of a plot against the Austrian Government leaked out, but the warning reached the Government in an inaccurate form and too late. On 25 July the Nazi conspirators drove into the Chancellery disguised in Army uniform, rushed up the great staircase into the room where Dollfuss had been conferring with Major Fey and several others, and shot Dollfuss at point-blank range. They left him to bleed to death for four hours and refused to accede to his requests for a priest. Meanwhile, although outwardly everything in Vienna appeared quite normal, news of the plot reached the Austrian President on holiday in Carinthia, and he at once ordered the Heimwehr to surround the Chancellery. After a long parley with Major Fey, who had been held as a hostage all this time by the Nazis, the conspirators were offered a safe conduct out of Austria *provided no blood was shed*, but directly it was learned that Dollfuss had been murdered, the safe-conduct was rescinded. The conspirators were captured and their leaders were executed by order of Kurt Schuschnigg, who succeeded Dollfuss as Chancellor. Hitler, for once frightened at the failure of the plot and at the energetic reaction of Mussolini, who had immediately massed an army on the Brenner, lay low and disclaimed all knowledge of it.

And so to the last act of the tragedy of the First Austrian Republic, culminating in those supremely dramatic days of March 1938 before Austria was wiped off the map of Europe.

The prospects confronting the new Chancellor were enough to daunt the most experienced statesman. The whole country was threatened with Civil War, the new Constitution was not yet three months old, the Fatherland Front was still immature, and the small Austrian army was dispersed and insufficient to cope with any considerable outbreak. Schuschnigg's only support was an Italian army camped on the Brenner. For the next three years he steered Austria through the most difficult times she had yet had to face. There was no outside help on which he could rely. Italy, after her Abyssinian adventure, was steadily growing weaker, year by year; France was more often without a Government than with one; and Great Britain appeared at the time to take no interest in Central Europe at all. If Austria was to survive, it would have to be by her own efforts.

Schuschnigg's first declaration of policy to his countrymen was an announcement that he desired a more democratic regime while still honouring the tradition of Seipel and Dollfuss. At first he did not have an easy passage at all. He was relatively inexperienced in political matters, and was at a disadvantage in his negotiations abroad in that at the time he knew little English. He visited London in 1935 but encountered such a frigid reception from the Labour Party, who labelled him as one of the men who had organised the bombardment of the Socialist tenement blocks in Vienna the year before, that he was not tempted to repeat the visit. In Paris he fared little better. Mussolini he had already visited the year before, and had taken an immediate dislike to him (which the Duce reciprocated). So for the next year he wisely concentrated on internal affairs, and in 1935, a year which passed off comparatively peacefully, he ordered the final disbandment of the Heimwehr.

Schuschnigg's task was certainly not made any easier by the wily intrigues of the new Nazi envoy to Austria "with a special mission" — Franz von Papen. This "special mission" was in reality to be the smoothing out of all obstacles in the way of the complete Nazi occupation of Austria. And so von Papen began his campaign of bland intrigue and honeyed words — adopting at first a policy of attrition and hoping to wear down Schuschnigg's

142

resistance. Hitler had instructed Papen to get Schuschnigg prepared for an agreement at all costs. He knew that Italy could never again be strong enough to mass an army on the Brenner as she had done two years previously. He knew that no other country was in a position to lift a finger to save Austria once Italy was neutralised — it was just a question of lulling his victim into a false sense of security before pouncing.

At this point it is advisable to be quite clear as to why Hitler wanted Austria. He was undisputed master of the German Reich with its 65 millions — he had just re-occupied the Rhineland without any opposition: why should he want Austria, a small country of only 6.5 millions? The reasons were partly psychological and partly strategic. During his early days in Vienna Hitler had been thrown into contact with Slavs and Jews, and as the years went by his hatred of them became an obsession. Moreover, anti-Slav feeling had always been stronger in Vienna than in Germany — indeed, Germany had at one time made a treaty with Russia (and was to make another one in 1939).

Hitler's reasons for wanting Austria were : —

(1) Personal revenge for his unhappy youth as a house-painter,
(2) Austria's gold reserves and mineral wealth,
(3) Austria had always been the key to South East Europe,
(4) Austria was a strategic essential for his designs on Czechoslovakia.

In other words, Hitler didn't underrate the importance of Vienna in Europe. The Western democracies did. And so Papen gradually won Schuschnigg over to the advisability of a "lasting" agreement with Germany by persuading him that Hitler was in such difficulties on his home front that he needed a diplomatic success for reasons of prestige.

"Offer him an agreement," purred Papen, "and he'll probably agree to the liquidation of the Austrian Nazis." Schuschnigg went to consult Mussolini, who agreed enthusiastically (of course), and Schuschnigg on his side was, as always, ready to go to almost any lengths to secure the freedom and independence of his country. An agreement was clearly a possibility, and in July 1936 it came:

(a) Hitler recognised full Austrian sovereignty.
(b) Each country agreed not to interfere in the internal affairs of the other.
(c) Austria was to conduct her policy on the basis of considering herself "a German State".

These were the three "open" clauses of the agreement — but how much did Hitler's recognition of Austria cost? What price had Schuschnigg to pay? He had to agree to include two crypto-Nazis in his Cabinet; he had to agree to an amnesty for all Nazi prisoners in Austria; and he had to agree to the free use of the Nazi greeting in private. All he got in exchange was the lifting of the 1000 Marks visa fee, and a vague promise to avoid provocative films and broadcasts.

The Pact was welcomed in Europe and Schuschnigg was held to have done well. But he was probably under no illusions as to what was coming. He knew that from now on there would be no help from outside and that he would have to fight his battle alone, and although he set out to observe scrupulously the terms of the agreement, the Nazis kept up the pressure remorselessly. By the middle of 1937 there were four Nazis in the Government, but despite these appeasements the Nazi commotion when the German Foreign Minister von Neurath visited Vienna was more violent than ever. Once more Schuschnigg went to Mussolini for advice, and Mussolini rather distantly gave him the usual comfortable assurance, which coming from him at this stage meant precisely nothing.

And so to February 1938, when, after months of discussion with Papen and members of his Cabinet, Schuschnigg consented to go to meet Hitler at Berchtesgaden. Like a later visitor to the same place he sincerely imagined that it would be possible to negotiate honourably with Hitler, for had not Papen assured him of "the protection of the Führer's glittering and immaculate word of honour"? It was exceedingly difficult for Schuschnigg with his complete integrity to understand that there could be people of German blood who had no conception of honour and truth at all.

So to Berchtesgaden he went, apprehensively, but determined to resist any encroachment on Austrian independence. He knew that the interview would be no fireside chat, but he can have had little idea of what was actually in store for him. His first shock was to find the heads of the German fighting forces ranged behind Hitler, and on the table a copy of the Austrian Defence Plan. His next was to find Hitler at his most frenzied. For hours the Führer raved and cursed, and when Schuschnigg, who was a heavy smoker, reached for a cigarette Hitler shrieked at him that he did not allow smoking in his presence. Slowly and coolly Schuschnigg lit his cigarette with raised eyebrows, tossed the match on to Hitler's table, and waited. On and on went the Führer, with a brief interval for a meagre lunch, until by late afternoon the full plan was clear. Austria was to be crushed by armed force forthwith unless:

(1) Key positions in the Austrian Cabinet were given to Nazis, such as Vice-Chancellor, War, Home Security, Foreign Affairs.
(2) Austria followed the anti-Czech policy of Germany.
(3) Anti-Semitic legislation was introduced.
(4) Austria left the League of Nations.
(5) A Currency Union was formulated.

145

In return for all this and more Hitler graciously undertook to respect Austrian independence (which he had already promised in 1936!).

Schuschnigg fought Hitler point by point, refusing to act without the authority of his President. For eleven hours he had been subjected without warning to the most abject humiliations and when he arrived back in Vienna next day he had no illusions left. Now at last he too saw his adversary clearly.

After consultation with his Ministers, and in order to save bloodshed, he accepted Hitler's terms, but with little confidence that they would be respected. Now that his eyes were at last open, Schuschnigg found himself. He knew that he was alone. Mussolini had abandoned him, France was as usual without a Government, and when he tried to get in touch with the British Government they were giving a reception to the German Foreign Minister Joachim von Ribbentrop and had no time to attend to him. Alone, he determined to face the storm. In a fighting speech on 24 February he roused Parliament to enthusiasm with a patriotic and highly emotional appeal for national unity, proving conclusively that Austria's economy and finances had never been sounder, and that Austria had no need of German "help". After the speech he received an ovation from a densely-packed crowd all along Vienna's Ringstrasse. This was his finest hour; now at last he did have a united Austria behind him, the Socialists promising him their support in a mass meeting at Floridsdorf on 7 March. And finally, Otto Habsburg, in an extraordinary letter from exile in Belgium, offered to take over the Chancellorship if called upon; an offer which Schuschnigg very respectfully turned down, because he knew that the arrival of a Habsburg could only add fuel to the flames. Later on perhaps, but not now.

By 9 March Schuschnigg was ready to launch his secret project which he had been preparing ever since his return from Berchtesgaden. Travelling to Innsbruck, the capital of his native Tyrol, he made the finest speech of his career, in the course of which he announced to a wildly cheering crowd of twenty thousand or so thronging the square below that a plebiscite would be held throughout Austria in three days' time: "Are you for a free and German, an independent and social, a Christian and united Austria?" In three days' time: and there are many communities in Austria which are more than twelve hours by train from Vienna. Yet the plebiscite had to be held immediately if Nazi interference was to be avoided.

Europe held its breath: even Hitler *must* realise that a freely held plebiscite would result in at least a 75% majority for Schuschnigg. Probably, then, Hitler would do something about it.

Events now moved fast to a climax. There was consternation in the Nazi camp and frantic appeals for instructions were sent to Berlin. The plebiscite was to be held on 13 March, and on 11 March two of the Nazis in the Austrian Government, acting on instructions from Berlin and backed by the imminent threat of German invasion, presented themselves at the Chancellery and demanded the cancellation of the plebiscite. Furthermore, Schuschnigg was to resign and appoint Arthur Seyss-Inquart Chancellor. Obviously this was the end; further resistance was hopeless. The tiny Austrian army was dispersed and inadequately equipped and had very few first-line aircraft. In a farewell broadcast Schuschnigg took his leave of the Austrian people telling them that he had ordered the Austrian army to offer no resistance to the invading Germans in order to avoid bloodshed. "God save Austria" were his last words as he turned away from the microphone.

On 12 March the German army was on its way and Hitler had got as far as Linz in its wake. The next day he entered Vienna, with the Gestapo of course, amid scenes of delirious enthusiasm, especially from the unemployed.

Schuschnigg, to the embarrassment of the "Führer", refused to abandon his people and passed into captivity with them. (Meanwhile, one remote Tyrol village, hearing nothing of these events, is said to have duly carried out its plebiscite, which resulted in a 98% majority for Schuschnigg.)

As the Gestapo got to work thousands of Austrians perished and thousands more were arrested, until at last Austria was considered fit for the honour of becoming just Gau VIII of the German Reich. Vienna, which had been the cultural centre of Europe, the reservoir of all the creative forces of the German-speaking people, became a shabby provincial city, and Austria itself literally ceased to exist. Even the name "Oesterreich" was abolished, and the country was degraded to the status of the "Ostmark", the Eastern Province originally set up by Charlemagne 1150 years previously. — The wheel of history had turned full circle. — Finis Austriae?

CHAPTER NINE

The Second Austrian Republic, 1945 to the present day

Austria	Elsewhere
1943 The Moscow Declaration.	
1945 April 13: The Russians capture Vienna.	1945 April: Death of Franklin D. Roosevelt who is succeeded by Harry S. Truman.
April 27: Declaration of Independence and Provisional Govt. under Karl Renner.	
April 27; *First post-war Philharmonic Concert.*	May: Execution of Mussolini, Death of Hitler.
Austrian Radio back on the air.	June: Foundation of the United Nations.
May: End of World War II in Europe.	August: Atomic bomb on Hiroshima.
July: *First post-war Salzburg Festival.*	Clement Attlee succeeds Winston Churchill as British Prime Minister.
November: First post-war General Election in Austria: Leopold Figl (People's Party) Chancellor.	Death of Lloyd George.
1946 September: Gruber-de Gasperi agreement on South Tyrol.	
The first Bregenz Festival.	
1946–55 Interminable negotiations on a State Treaty for Austria.	
1947 Marshall Aid (E. R. P.)	1947 The "New Look".
1948 *Death of Franz Lehár.*	1948 Murder of Gandhi.
1949 *Death of Richard Strauss.*	
Austria joins UNESCO.	1950 *Death of Bernard Shaw.*
1950 Death of Karl Renner.	1951 Winston Churchill succeeds Clement Attlee as British Prime Minister.
1951 *Death of Arnold Schönberg.*	
First post-war Festival of Vienna.	
1952 *Re-opening of St. Stephen's Cathedral in Vienna.*	1952 Death of George VI and accession of Queen Elizabeth II.
	1953 Death of Stalin.
	Dwight D. Eisenhower President of the U.S.A.

Austria	*Elsewhere*
1955 15 May: Signature of the State Treaty in Vienna. 19 September: Last of the occupation troops leave Austria. 26 Oct.: Neutrality Act. Austria admitted to U.N. *Re-opening of the Opera House, the Burgtheater and the Spanish Riding School.*	1955 Anthony Eden succeeds Winston Churchill as British Prime Minister.
	1956 Uprising in Hungary.
1957 Adolf Schärf President.	1957 *Death of Arturo Toscanini.*
1959 Austria joins EFTA. The South Tyrol question before the United Nations.	
1961 Vienna meeting Kennedy-Khruschev.	1961 John F. Kennedy President of the United States.
1963 *Re-constitution of Salzburg University.*	1963 Assassination of John F. Kennedy. L. B. Johnson succeeds as President.
1965 Franz Jonas President.	1965 Death of Winston Churchill.
	1967 The "six-day war" between Israelis and Arabs.
	1968 Richard Nixon President of the U.S.A. Troops of the Warsaw Pact countries intervene in Czechoslovakia.
	1969 Neil Armstrong is the first man on the moon.
1970 Bruno Kreisky Chancellor.	
1972 *400th anniversary of the Spanish Riding School.*	
1974 Rudolf Kirchschläger President.	1974 Resignation of President Nixon who is succeded by Gerald Ford.
1975 *Death of Robert Stolz.*	
1979 Ratification of SALT II by US-President Carter and Breschnjew in Vienna.	1979 Margaret Thatcher (Great Britain) first woman for Prime Minister in Europe. Revolution in Persia.
	1980 Ronald Reagan President of the U.S.A.
1982 First visit of Ex-Empress Zita to Austria.	1982 Falkland War. War in Lebanon.

Finis Austriae — or so the Nazi masters of Germany thought. In actual fact however Austria was still very much alive in the hearts of loyal subjects in the Resistance, in the concentration camps, or in exile. The Austrian resistance movement started up as soon as Hitler's troops entered Austria, and comprised people of all ages, parties and classes. Acts of conspiracy and sabotage may well have seemed futile in view of the Gestapo's vigilance, as any suspicion of resistance was put down with remorseless brutality; yet the resistance movement remained in being throughout the war and even included elements in the armed forces.

By and large however Hitler's reception by the Austrian people in March 1938 was rapturous, or perhaps delirious would be a more appropriate word in view of the rude awakening that delirium is sometimes followed by. In the first few months Hitler was regarded as a Saviour. Unemployment was practically eliminated thanks to the vast new armaments programme, including the great steelworks at Linz and the aircraft factories at Wiener Neustadt, and jobs were progressively easier to get as the liquidation of the Jews got under way. But in time the jubilation began to evaporate, especially when it became apparent that all the best jobs were going to Germans, and despite all the heady victories of 1939 and 1940 the German invasion of Russia in 1941 sent a shudder through the older generation, who knew only too well what war in the Russian winter was like. It was after Stalingrad, where two divisions consisting mainly of Austrians were wiped out, that Austrian morale touched rock bottom, and only secret listeners to the BBC could be heartened by the Declaration following the meeting of the Allied Foreign Ministers in Moscow on 1 November 1943:

"The Governments of the United Kingdom, the Soviet Union and the United States of America are agreed that Austria, the first country to fall a victim to Hitlerite aggression, shall be liberated from German domination. They regard the annexation imposed on Austria by Germany on 15 March 1938 as null and void ... Austria is reminded however that ... in the final settlement account will inevitably be taken of her own contribution to her liberation."

This last sentence may well have weighed on Austrian minds as the Russian armies fought their way into Austria from the east, and the British and United States forces were closing in from the south and west respectively. During the fighting in and around Vienna a group of Austrian patriots in German uniforms managed to get in touch with the Russian forces in the hope of sparing Vienna the devastation that had been meted out to Budapest. Local resistance movements were also in active operation in the Provinces, notably in Carinthia, Styria, Tyrol and Vorarlberg.

The liberation of Vienna was completed on 13 April 1945, and of all Austrian territory by 27 April. On this very same day the leaders of the three main political parties at the time, the newly constituted People's Party (the successors of the former Christian-Socials), the Socialist Party and the Communist Party issued from Vienna a joint Declaration of Independence to the effect that:

(1) The democratic Republic of Austria is re-established and the Constitution of 1920 is to be re-enacted.
(2) The Anschluss imposed upon the people of Austria in 1938 is null and void.

The Constitution in question is, briefly, that of a Federal Republic, with a President elected by direct suffrage for a term of 6 years, and two Houses of Parliament, an Upper

House (Bundesrat) with the right of veto, and a Lower House (Nationalrat). The Government for many years was a Coalition between the People's Party, which has won a majority of the seats at every post-war election and therefore supplied the Federal Chancellor, and the Socialist party, which supplied the Vice-Chancellor. Each of the nine Federal Provinces has its own Provincial Government for local legislation.

A Provisional Government was set up on 27 April under Karl Renner, the same Karl Renner as had risen to a similar occasion in 1918. This Government, which included 7 Communists, was for the time being recognised only by the Soviet Union, the three Western Powers withholding recognition on the grounds that it was a matter for all the four Allies, that no Allied Commission had yet been set up, and that the three Western Powers had still not been granted access to Vienna. Some ten weeks later an outline agreement was reached in London on the form the Allied occupation of Austria was to take. The country was to be divided into four zones, a Soviet Zone consisting of Lower Austria (excluding Vienna), Burgenland, and all Upper Austria north of the Danube; an American Zone of the Province of Salzburg, and Upper Austria south of the Danube; a British Zone of Styria and Carinthia; and a French Zone of Tyrol and Vorarlberg. As for Vienna, each of the four Powers was allotted a sector of the city, the Inner City, or First District, being under quadripartite control. Movement between the different sectors of Vienna was free, but to cross from one Zone to another identity cards in four languages (and with over a dozen official stamps) were needed, even by members of the Allied forces. The latter were also restricted to certain routes out of Vienna, American and French personnel to the main road or railway to Linz, and British personnel to the Semmering road or railway. An inadequately stamped pass or travel document meant being turned back at the boundary of the Russian Zone, which was an almost everyday occurrence.

By 1 September 1945 small parties of Allied representatives had at last been admitted to Vienna, and the Allied Council had met for the first time on 11 September.

The condition of Vienna was pitiful indeed. During the last weeks of the fighting three of the city's most cherished possessions were almost totally destroyed. On 12 March the Opera had been burnt out in an air raid; it had been closed ever since the Nazis decreed "total war" in June 1944, the final performance being appropriately enough "Götterdämmerung". On 12 April the Burgtheater was destroyed, and the same day St. Stephen's Cathedral was in flames, little being left standing except the outside walls and the west front. By some miracle the great tower, though severely damaged, stood firm. There was complete chaos everywhere. Transport was virtually non-existent, and it was impossible to tell when the few trams that were managing to operate would reach their destination in view of the constant and unpredictable power-cuts. If the lights went on all over Europe in that spring of 1945 there was very little light in Vienna. As for the food situation, it is perhaps indicated most vividly by a list of commodities, published in the Press (or what there was of it) that the Red Army was presenting to the people of Vienna: it was emphasised that the list contained salt. When at last a rationing scheme could be worked out, the daily ration in Vienna dwindled at one time to a precarious 800 calories, and before the end of 1945 the Allied Council had to apply to UNRRA for immediate assistance. At first, the only food supplies were what had been left behind by the retreating Germans, but as there was no transport to move them, the local black marketeers had things very much their own way. 41% of the railways and 66% of the rolling-stock had been destroyed, as well as over 50% of the Danube shipping. Normal commercial transactions were ruled out as nobody would accept money. Banknotes were mere scraps of paper, and a good wad of foreign currency was needed for furtive transactions in unlit doorways or unsavoury night-spots run by black marketeers with loaves of bread or an ounce or two of flour to offer. The most persuasive currency of all of course was cigarettes.

In the countryside the food situation was slightly less catastrophic, the main problem being the lack of transport. Most of the market towns were littered with debris and craters, and the roads were blocked by milling masses of "Displaced Persons," returning soldiers, foreign workers, ex-inmates of concentration camps, and refugees who could not make up their minds who they had most to fear from, the Russians or the Germans.

Yet despite all the misery and material hardships there was an atmosphere of relief and resilience as all able-bodied sections of the population, under-nourished as they were, got down to the job of clearing up the mess. It was as if a long and lurid nightmare had been broken. And this being Austria, one of the sturdiest of the new post-war growths was music, even among the ruins. As early as 27 April, with the war still in its final throes, the Vienna Philharmonic gave its first post-war concert and the Austrian Radio was back on the air; and on 1 May the State Opera gave its first performance in the virtually undamaged Volksoper. On the very same day as all the German forces in Italy and Western Austria surrendered, most of Vienna's theatres that were still habitable announced their re-opening. Lectures were even started in the badly damaged University. In the Provinces too music and the arts followed hard on the heels of the retreating armies. By mid-July the Graz Opera and Playhouse were both open, and in August lectures were got under way at Innsbruck University. In Salzburg the first post-war Festival was launched under the patronage of the General Officer Commanding US troops in Europe, the programme being a ludicrously

modest one by today's standards: Mozart's "Die Ent-
führung" and Hofmannsthal's "Der Tor und der Tod".
In Vienna, the great musical event of 1945 was the performance of Beethoven's "Fidelio" on 6 October with
which the State Opera moved into its provisional quarters
at the Theater an der Wien, the very same theatre as had
seen the first performance of the very same opera during
Napoleon's occupation of Vienna. No one who was present
will forget the tide of emotion that swept through the house
at the great Chorus at the end of Act I when the prisoners,
groping their way out of the darkness of confinement,
acclaim their new-found liberty. It was almost too topical.

Gradually, very gradually, thanks to the almost superhuman efforts of the Austrian population, the rubble was
cleared, order was restored, and life began to return to
some semblance of normality. Politically, the Allied Council
gave its approval to a big step forward on 20 October by
approving the extension of the Provisional Government's
authority to cover the whole country, and a month later
the first post-war General Election was held (in a country
under military occupation by four different Powers),
the outcome being a Coalition between the People's
Party, with 85 seats, and the Socialists with 76, the number
of Communists declining to 4. In his first speech in the
newly elected Nationalrat, and his last as Chancellor before
being elected Austria's first post-war President, Karl
Renner dwelt on the difficulties of organising an efficient
civil administration alongside the Military Governments
of the four occupying Powers: it was like, he said, trying
to row a small boat with four elephants as passengers.
The People's party having won the election, Renner was
therefore succeeded as Chancellor by Leopold Figl, who
for the next ten years, either as Chancellor or as Foreign
Minister, kept his gaze steadfastly fixed on Austria's
primary objective, the ending of the occupation and the
regaining of national sovereignty.

The new Government's first step was to curb inflation by bringing the circulation of banknotes under control and reintroducing the Schilling instead of the wartime Mark. Economically, Austria was kept going by massive aid under the Marshall Plan to the tune of 1 milliard dollars up till the end of 1953. By no means the least influential factor in Marshall Aid was its psychological effect. It gave the Austrian people confidence in the good intentions of the West, showed them that Austria had not been written off by the free world, and was a powerful stimulant to the work of reconstruction. As for the political situation, from the Austrian Government's point of view it was one long frustration, as agreement in the Allied Council on any matter of importance was a nine-days' wonder. The first ray of hope was not vouchsafed until the end of 1946, when at the New York Conference of Foreign Ministers their Deputies were instructed to draft a State Treaty. Little did they know that it was to be another eight and a half years before a State Treaty was at long last agreed. Between May and October 1947, for instance, the State Treaty Committee set up by the Moscow Conference of Foreign Ministers in April 1947 held no fewer than 85 abortive meetings, progress being blocked by Russian insistence on the discussion of various alien and intractable issues, such as Yugoslav claims and Trieste, which had nothing whatever to do with the Austrian Treaty. At last, in desperation the Austrian Foreign Minister Karl Gruber requested the Brazilian Government in 1952 to bring the matter of an Austrian Treaty before the United Nations, where a resolution was adopted appealing to the Four Powers to arrive at an agreement. The Eastern bloc however abstained from voting and disputed the United Nations' authority to intervene in the Austrian question at all.

The February 1953 meeting of the Foreign Ministers' Deputies charged with drafting a State Treaty was their 260th and was as fruitless as the previous 259. The next red herring was Russian insistence at the February 1954 Berlin Conference of Foreign Ministers on postponing the departure of occupation forces from Austria until the conclusion of a Treaty with Germany. The Russian Foreign Minister Molotov also proposed that Austria should adopt a policy of neutrality, to which the Western representatives replied that to hang neutrality round Austria's neck like a symbol of servitude was to make a mockery of Austrian sovereignty, of which the Soviet Union was one of the sponsors. A voluntary assumption of neutrality on the other hand would be a different matter altogether, and this Austria readily agreed to.

Even so, it was not until 1955 that the deadlock was broken by a development that gave Austria some cause for cautious optimism after so many disappointments. What happened was that the aftermath of Stalin's death began to thaw out the State Treaty negotiations. By March 1955 Russia had agreed to abandon her insistence on coupling the State Treaty with a German Peace Treaty. In return, Austria confirmed her voluntary assumption of a policy of neutrality. Accordingly, on 24 March Molotov invited Julius Raab, the new Austrian Chancellor, to head an Austrian delegation to Moscow, and the proposal was duly approved by the Western Allies. The delegation, which included Leopold Figl as Foreign Minister, negotiated in Moscow from 12—15 April and on 14 April a dramatic message from Chancellor Julius Raab was received in Vienna: "Austria will be free: every inch of our native soil is to be restored to us and all prisoners of war will be on their way home."

Throughout Austria the expectancy was positively electric; after 17 years of captivity, devastation, hunger and occupation freedom was no longer a mirage. The Austrian delegation's return from Moscow was like a triumphal progress; and then came the great day, 15 May 1955, when the State Treaty was ceremonially signed in the Belvedere and the Foreign Ministers (Molotov, Macmillan, Dulles, Pinay and Figl) came out on to the balcony and a radiant Leopold Figl held up the Treaty for every member of the vast throng in the garden below to get at least a glimpse of — Austria was free, the long agony was over.

The last foreign soldier left Austrian territory on 19 September, and on 26 October the Nationalrat unanimously voted a Neutrality Act stipulating that Austria would not join any bloc or military alliance, and would not permit foreign military bases on her territory. Neutrality has been the corner-stone of Austrian policy ever since, and will continue to be rigidly adhered to in all circumstances.

There could be no more fitting epilogue to the Austrian State Treaty than the words of the American Secretary of State John Foster Dulles after the signing:

> "Today it is decided that Austria will resume its place as a free and independent nation. It would be possible in a sense to say that this freedom and independence is being conferred. It would, however, be far more accurate to say that the freedom and independence have been won by the Austrian people themselves. Seventeen years ago the independence of Austria was lost to what then seemed to be overwhelming power. But in this case, as is indeed always the case, military power succumbed to the moral power of an ideal. The Austrian people have never lost the vision of a free and independent Austria and their words and deeds have consistently reflected a solemn resolve that that vision should become a reality. So today the Austrian people can rejoice, not because of what has been given them but because of what they have won for themselves.

Today, as the Austrian people rejoice, the people of America rejoice with them. That is not only because the American people know and have long admired the Austrian people, but because that admiration now takes on new scope and greater depth. Today we feel indebted to the Austrian people because they have brought about a fresh example of what the United Nations Charter refers to as respect for the principle of equal rights and self-determination of peoples."

Economically, the Treaty imposed daunting obligations: Austria undertook to deliver to Russia 1 million tons of oil a year from the Lower Austrian oilfields for the next 10 years; to deliver to Russia over the next 6 years goods to the value of 150 million dollars as payment for the return of some 400 undertakings confiscated by Russia as constituting "former German assets"; and to pay Russia 2 million dollars for the return of Austrian interests in the Danube Shipping Co. Once these obligations had been faithfully and punctually discharged the Austrian economy went ahead by leaps and bounds, one of its most lucrative items being an all-the-year round tourist trade which is still going strong.

Culturally too 1955 was an "annus mirabilis", culminating in the re-opening of the Spanish Riding School, the Burgtheater, and the Opera House all within the space of a few months.

Politically, Austria seems at last to have come out into calm water since the signing of the State Treaty. Governments succeed one another every four years or so, politicians come and go, but for the first twenty years after World War II the results of every election remained substantially the same — a Coalition between the two main parties, the right-wing People's Party which supplied the Chancellor because it had the most seats, and the Socialist

Party which supplied the Vice-Chancellor. Government and other official posts were allotted on proportion to the relative strengths of the two parties in the Coalition. It was a system that made for an element of political stability and obviated the mistakes and upheavals of the First Republic; but on the other hand it tended to stultify political initiative and enterprise. It also meant that there was no appreciable opposition in Parliament: policy was worked out beforehand by the Chancellor and his two-party Cabinet, and Parliament obediently ratified it. It was not until the March 1966 Election that one of the parties, the People's Party, succeeded in winning an overall majority and was able to form a Government on its own, with the Socialists constituting a strong and healthy opposition in Parliament. But at the next General Election in March 1970 neither of the two main parties managed to persuade the electorate to give it an overall majority.

On the international stage, Austria has done her best to pull her weight in the various United Nations welfare organisations she has been a member of since being admitted to the United Nations in 1955. Full membership of the European Common Market being deemed incompatible with obligations written into the State Treaty, Austria had to look around for access to some other supra-national market, and therefore put her signature to the EFTA agreement which came into force in May 1960. Membership of EFTA, though neither able nor intended to serve as a substitute for some sort of association with the Common Market, has at least averted the danger of Austria's economic isolation. But in view of Austria's trade-pattern, some sort of special relationship with the Common Market short of actual membership, and without infringing neutrality and other international obligations, seems imperative, and negotiations to this end have been proceeding in Brussels for over 4 years; it was in December 1961 that the first application for an exclusively economic association was made by the Austrian Foreign Minister.

Relations with foreign countries have been, with two exceptions, consistently friendly. With Hungary, relations were clouded for a while by the Hungarian uprising of 1956, during which no fewer than 170,000 refugees poured across Austria's eastern frontier, and political relations with Italy have been sorely strained by the intractable and eternal problem of South Tyrol.

It will be recalled that the secret Treaty of London in 1915 promised Italy South Tyrol up to the Brenner Pass in return for entering World War I on the side of the Allies. Accordingly, at the Peace Conference in 1919 Italy presented the bill, having previously taken the precaution of occupying the territory in question. England and France were bound by the Treaty, President Wilson was not; and at first he came out strongly against the transfer. He was in an agonising dilemma: on the one hand, his own doctrine of self-determination, on the other the Treaty promises, the "strategic security" of Italy, and last but by no means least the Italian vote in the USA. So eventually he withdrew his objections and South Tyrol passed to Italian sovereignty. It was a decision he bitterly regretted in later years, describing it as a "great mistake", and in his Memoirs of the Peace Conference the British Prime Minister David Lloyd George admitted that the transfer of South Tyrol was incompatible with the principle of self-determination which was implicitly embodied in the original Allied war aims.

Without ever having recourse to an active irredentist policy to recover this lovely land, Austria has not hesitated to enlist world opinion in favour of repairing the manifest injustice of the transfer. By what is loosely referred to as "South Tyrol" is meant the predominantly German-speaking territory from the Brenner pass down to the Salurn Gorge about half way between Bolzano and Trento, an

162

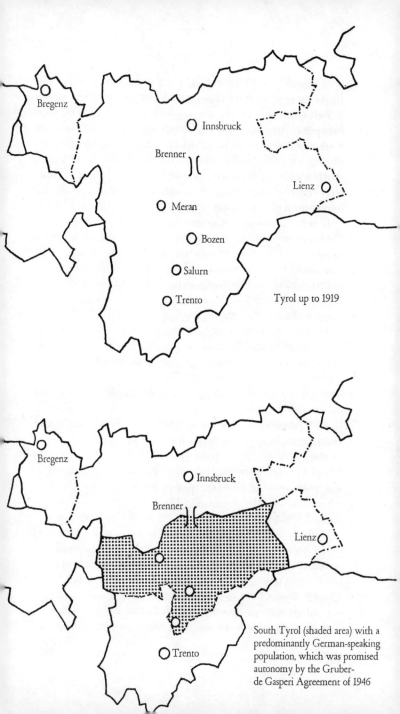

Bregenz

Innsbruck

Brenner }{

Lienz

Meran

Bozen

Salurn

Trento

Tyrol up to 1919

Bregenz

Innsbruck

Brenner

Lienz

Trento

South Tyrol (shaded area) with a
predominantly German-speaking
population, which was promised
autonomy by the Gruber-
de Gasperi Agreement of 1946

area roughly corresponding to the Italian Province of Bolzano. The first census carried out in this area, under Italian control and after the transfer, showed 223,000 German-speaking and Ladinean inhabitants (the Ladineans are a small Rheto-Romanic group who have survived in some of the South-Tyrol valleys) and only 20,000 Italians. Accordingly, as soon as Mussolini came to power in Italy the German-language schools were closed and the German language was done away with in all public offices; and in 1939 an agreement between Hitler and Mussolini offered the German-speaking inhabitants of South Tyrol the option of moving to new homes in the German Reich. This nefarious transaction was of course tantamount to the abandonment of South Tyrol to Italy: nefarious, because Hitler, in return for Mussolini's inaction during Hitler's annexation of Austria 1938, was presenting his partner in crime with a territory that did not belong to him anyway. So immediately after World War II the Provisional Austrian Government asked for a plebiscite in South Tyrol, but the London Conference of Foreign Ministers decided in October 1945, mainly in deference to the wishes of the United States Government (for the same reason as in 1919, the Italian vote in the USA), not to make any major changes in boundaries at Italy's expense. Speaking in the House of Commons on 5 July 1946 Winston Churchill stated that the transfer of South Tyrol to Italy was one of the worst blots on the Treaty of St. Germain, and went on:

> "I know of no case in the whole of Europe more than that of Austrian Tyrol where the Atlantic Charter, and the subsequent Charter of the United Nations, might have been extended to its people. Why could not the natives of this beautiful land, the land of the patriot Andreas Hofer, be allowed to say a word about their own destiny? Why could they not have a fair and free plebiscite there under

the supervision of the Great Powers? Is it not illogical to have one standard of ethnic criteria for Trieste and Venezia Giulia and another for South Tyrol?"

And at the Peace Conference in Paris the British Foreign Secretary Ernest Bevin observed on 8 October 1946:

"We for our part were never altogether happy about leaving some 200,000 German-speaking people in Italy, and were anxious that the Italian Government should do everything to preserve the minority rights of the German-speaking inhabitants of South Tyrol."

Actually an agreement on local autonomy for South Tyrol was negotiated in 1946 between the Foreign Ministers of Austria and Italy, Karl Gruber and Alcide de Gasperi, and incorporated in the Italian Peace Treaty. But there has been a ceaseless wrangle between the Austrian and Italian Governments ever since, Austria accusing Italy of not having implemented, or even attempted to implement, the terms of the Gruber - de Gasperi Agreement. What was regarded as particularly sharp practice on Italy's part was her amalgamation of South Tyrol (i. e. the Province of Bolzano), which is overwhelmingly German-speaking, with the predominantly Italian Province of Trentino, thus forming a single "autonomous region" with an Italian majority. In 1960 and again in 1961 Austria brought the matter before the General Assembly of the United Nations, the only results being resolutions which were unanimous and ineffective. Since then there have been endless Commissions and Committees, and some deplorable terrorist outrages. The Foreign Ministers of Austria and Italy have enjoyed conversations in many of Europe's most picturesque and comfortable resorts, and issued cordial communiques thereafter, but for many years the concrete results were precisely nil. Eventually, and largely owing to Austrian persistence, a "package deal" satisfactuary to both parties was agreed towards the end of 1969.

With the problem of South Tyrol no longer simmering, the Republic of Austria nowadays pursues its tranquil course unmolested from without and unsubverted from within. The four factors that were mainly responsible for bringing the First Republic down were unemployment, political armies, interference from without, and lack of national confidence and patriotism. These are the mistakes and shortcomings that the Second Republic has so far managed to avoid. Passions are cooler now, political tensions on the whole less acute. There is no equivalent in present-day Austria of the old political armies, the Heimwehr and the Schutzbund. Public buildings are not burned down as in 1927. The old storms and stresses have abated; the past has been assimilated and digested. Austria's outstanding post-war statesmen, Karl Renner, Leopold Figl and Julius Raab, set the Second Republic on a course that their successors are wisely determined to follow. And above all, neutral Austria is at peace with her neighbours.